PIEMINISTER

LIVE & EAT PIE!

To Ned, Fina, Lorna, Lettie and all the other young pie people.
We'll always try to bake things better.

An Hachette UK Company
www.hachette.co.uk

First published in Great Britain in 2023 by Kyle Books,
an imprint of Octopus Publishing Group Limited
Carmelite House
50 Victoria Embankment
London EC4Y 0DZ
www.kylebooks.co.uk

ISBN: 978 1 80419 0630

All photography produced by Rob Wicks, apart from brand imagery
supplied by Pieminister on pages 7–9, 100–101, 115, 120, 166–167, 184.

Distributed in the US by Hachette Book Group,
1290 Avenue of the Americas, 4th and 5th Floors,
New York, NY 10104

Distributed in Canada by Canadian Manda Group,
664 Annette St., Toronto, Ontario, Canada M6S 2C8

Publisher: Joanna Copestick
Editor: Isabel Jessop
Copy Editor: Vicky Orchard
Art Director: Yasia Williams
Photography: Rob Wicks
Art Direction and Illustration: Ryan Thomas
Food Styling: Alison Clarkson
Co-writers: Romany Simon, Jeni Hunsley
Production: Emily Noto

Printed and bound in China

PIEMINISTER

LIVE & EAT PIE!

ETHICAL & SUSTAINABLE PIE MAKING

Tristan Hogg & Jon Simon

CONTENTS

ABBREVIATION KEY:

V = VEGETARIAN

VG = PLANT-BASED

VO = VEGETARIAN OPTION

VGO = PLANT-BASED OPTION

GFO = GLUTEN-FREE OPTION

INTRODUCTION

WELCOME TO OUR WONDERFUL, SUSTAINABLE WORLD OF PIES

Since we started Pieminister in 2003 we've aspired to be a sustainable business and in recent years we've really upped our game. Food production accounts for a shocking 25% of global greenhouse gas emissions, so, to be part of the solution and to focus our collective minds, we set some goals in 2020 to help us make the greatest, most positive impact for the sake of the planet.

A great thing about this goal setting at work is that it's flowed into our choices and actions at home. We see this book as a chance for us to share what we've learned more widely, alongside a raft of original pie recipes which all have two things in common; they're created with sustainable ingredients and they're insanely good to eat.

We're far from being the last word in sustainability and we defer to people who are far cleverer than us in this book. You'll gain loads of insight and inspiration from their contributions, as well as some amazing recipes they've kindly created with us.

We actively encourage you to freestyle with your piemaking depending on the time of year, your taste buds, or what needs using up in your kitchen. The way we've laid out the recipes reflects this, with tips and tricks to help you get creative.

We've also tried to untangle the truth from the myth among the recipes. From fighting food waste and finding truly deforestation-free fats for making pastry, to getting to grips with the mysterious world of recycling, this book is our sustainability story so far. It's one long learning curve that we're still navigating. We hope that by sharing what we've discovered, we can inspire you too, in the kitchen and beyond.

And just as importantly, we hope you enjoy baking these pies as much as we have.

TRISTAN & JON

OUR LIFE OF PIE

FROM THE VERY BEGINNING

JON:

I was born in Croydon, South London in 1972. I was a busy kid, always playing football, messing around on my BMX or looking for ways to earn money. I started my first business aged 12, washing cars for local cabbies. I soon realized valeting wasn't for me, so I offered my services as a delivery boy to the local greengrocer. Many more entrepreneurial endeavours followed, most of which involved long hours, low pay and pretending I knew what I was doing.

I left school with a couple of A levels and a circle of life-long friends. Then, following in the footsteps of Malcolm McLaren and Ray Davies I headed off to Croydon School of Art. This is where I hit my stride. I loved art and design and went on to Nottingham Trent University to study Furniture and Product design.

In the first week at uni, I met Romany, a fashion student who lived next door. Little did I know then that years later we'd be married with two kids and have started a pie business with her brother!

TRIS:

I was born in Birmingham in 1979. My parents moved a lot and soon we were living in Jeddah, Saudi Arabia, which I loved. Aged 10, we were back in England, in Bristol, where I enjoyed school, although I'm not sure school enjoyed me. I spent a lot of time in front of the headmaster or sneaking off to skateboard... At 15 (now in Cheshire), everyone agreed that it might be best if I left school and with a collective sigh of relief I headed to Broxton Hall, a country house hotel to learn to be a chef.

JON MEETS ROMANY

HAVE YOU SEEN THIS MAN?

JON:

At the same time, I'd finished uni and knew I wanted to run my own business – I just didn't know what. My ideas always led me towards food and hospitality, and I spent days at the local library researching everything from importing peanuts and olives to making energy sweets. It soon became clear that the most fun thing to do would be to open a bar. But I didn't have any money, so I got myself on to a TV game show, determined to win the cash prize. Six months later, I'd done it, winning *Wanted* on Channel 4, with enough money to put my plans into action. In June 1996, I opened my first bar in Clapham, South London, and within a month my girlfriend's brother Tristan had moved into the pub and was running the kitchen.

TRIS:

Training to be a chef in Cheshire was a revelation. I loved the fast pace and energy of it, but soon got tired of country life. So, I moved to London, to see if I could run a kitchen of my own – at my sister's boyfriend's new pub! This is where Jon and I became great friends and workmates.

Working together at the Circle Bar was amazing. I was 18, Jon was in his early 20s and Clapham was rocking. The bar was packed at the weekends and the parties were legendary.

JON:

At the time gastro pubs were almost unheard of; there was The Eagle in Farringdon and the Masons Arms in Battersea, and that was about it. Using these places as inspiration, we knocked the wall down between the bar and kitchen and Tristan started serving a new kind of pub grub: venison sausages and mash with redcurrant jus, lamb fillets on herb couscous, and possibly the best Sunday roast in London.

TRIS:

In between serving customers and having fun, we were experimenting with other food business ideas: takeaway soup tubs with par-baked bread, salad dressings, even flavoured vodkas which we served behind the bar. We talked about pies too – Jon had discovered a pie shop called Harry's Café de Wheels in Sydney while travelling around Australia and thought something similar might work in the UK. But then I got an offer I couldn't refuse.

JON:

One day a guy walked in and asked Tris if he'd like to travel the world cooking for rockstars – six weeks later we waved him off!

TRIS:

The next two years were a blur, but eventually I landed in Sydney where I stayed for a year, working at a smart restaurant overlooking Sydney Opera House. I'd learnt so much as a tour chef, but this took my skills to a new level. The people working there were some of the best and I soaked up every ounce of knowledge I could.

However, it wasn't all work and no play. I was making the most of the surf, sunshine and culinary delights that Sydney had to offer. One of which was their excellent pies! I was amazed how different they were; the flavours were adventurous, and they were enjoyed by everyone from surfers and skateboarders to cricket fans. The pastry was great too.

One day after a surf on Bondi Beach, I was eating a particularly good pie when the name Pieminister popped into my head. Remembering the conversations I'd had with Jon two years before and armed with plenty of energy and a great name for a new business, I headed back to the UK to pick up where we had left off and put our plans into action.

JON:

By early 2003 the Pieminister business plan was well underway! Working out how to make pies on a commercial level involved sourcing second-hand manufacturing equipment we didn't have a clue how to use. And experimenting with recipes in Tristan's mum's kitchen in Bristol. Slowly but surely, things started to come together.

A derelict printworks on Bristol's notorious Stokes Croft became Pieminister's bakery and café. Uni friends were enlisted to help with branding, photography and a website, and finally, in December 2003, after working 16-hour days for months on end, we opened for business.

JON'S SON NED

TRIS:

Day one, we sold 10 pies, and most of those were to my mum. Then we invited the local press along with the promise of a free pie, and within days the reviews were in, and they were good. A queue formed every lunchtime. Next came a stall at London's Borough Market, then requests to supply local pubs and restaurants started rolling in. Then along came Glastonbury...

OUR FIRST FESTIVAL

JON:

The Festival was a pivotal moment for us; everyone wanted one of our Mothership pie feasts, and within a couple of years, we were opening new restaurants, supplying fine food halls across the UK and exporting to Ireland and Holland.

TRIS:

We soon outgrew our Stokes Croft kitchens, moving up the road to the bigger bakery where we still make our pies to this day. Stokes Croft is still our spiritual home, with the café and offices as busy as ever!

We continue to be amazed on the success of the business and we are so grateful for the support we get from all our customers and suppliers. There have been so many highs and certainly some lows. We try not to talk about the squid pie, or the Pie Pod...

JON:

...or the restaurant we opened in Amsterdam!

TRIS:

...or some of the disasters we have encountered while trading at festivals. I once got a call at 3am, when one of the team drove a truck into the middle of pond on the outskirts of Dublin.

JON:

It's been a great adventure so far, we're still great friends, and we're super excited to be writing this next chapter in Pieminister's history.

ROMANY
JON'S WIFE & TRIS'S SISTER

IT'S NOT EASY BEING GREEN

IS IT JUST US OR IS SUSTAINABILITY ONE OF THOSE THINGS THAT THE MORE YOU TRY TO UNDERSTAND IT, THE MORE CONFUSED YOU FEEL?

And some of the stuff you discover just feels so big and unsurmountable?

WE KNOW WE NEED TO REDUCE THE AMOUNT OF BEEF AND DAIRY WE CONSUME...

...but small-scale farming with grazing animals can actually be beneficial in terms of soil health and biodiversity.

However, there's not enough land to produce the amount of grass-fed meat we currently consume. So yes, we still need to reduce the amount we eat.

WE KNOW WE NEED TO SOURCE AS LOCALLY AS WE CAN

But does this disproportionately create water stress on one country, and would it be better to share the strain?

but a tomato that has been shipped from Spain to the UK is likely to be more sustainable than out-of-season British tomatoes grown in a heated polytunnel.

DON'T SHOP LOCAL!

AND PLANT-BASED ISN'T ALWAYS BETTER...

A veggie burger made from soy grown in South America has likely contributed to the devastation of rainforest, and much of the palm oil in our foods is linked to deforestation too...

...but simply switching to a different oil like coconut could just make the situation worse...

AND ACTUALLY SOME PALM OIL IS FAR BETTER FOR THE PLANET THAN MOST BUTTER!

THEN THERE'S PACKAGING. WE SHOULD TRY TO AVOID PLASTIC TO SAVE OUR SEAS AND MARINE LIFE.

But a paper bag has a much bigger carbon footprint than a reused plastic bag.

NEW BIODEGRADABLE PLASTICS SOUND BETTER FOR THE PLANET, RIGHT?

But the proper infrastructure to recycle bioplastics is limited in the UK and they cause big problems if they end up in conventional plastic recycling or in landfill...

SO ISN'T THIS WORSE THAN PLASTIC THEN!? IT'S COMPLICATED ISN'T IT.

BUT LET'S ALL TAKE A DEEP BREATH AND FOLLOW A FEW SIMPLE STEPS WHICH WE KNOW WILL LEAD US IN THE RIGHT DIRECTION.

DO THE PIE THING

- If you do eat meat or dairy, source local and pasture-fed, free range or organic. Eat the best you can afford and save it for special occasions.
- If you eat anything containing palm oil, make sure it's certified sustainable palm oil. Ideally Identity preserved (see more on page 30).
- Make a few shopping changes to create less packaging waste. It's not all or nothing.
- Do everything in your power to avoid food waste.
- Spend wisely and support farmers, shops and smallholders doing the right thing, near or far.

FROM A PIE-GONE ERA

YOU DON'T KNOW WHAT YOU'VE GOT 'TIL IT'S GONE:
A FACT THAT FAR TOO MANY PIE LOVERS
HAVE LEARNED THE HARD WAY.

For those of you still hankering after a pie from menus past, here's an
index of your most-missed 'RIPies'. Use it to find the near-as-dammit recipes
right here in this book to enjoy Pieminister pies gone by.

MINTY LAMB
SEE PAGE 154
R.I.Pie 2014

BEEFY COSSACK
SEE PAGE 34
R.I.Pie 2007

SMOKIN' BBQ
SEE PAGE 130
R.I.Pie 2021

MIGHTY APHRODITE
SEE PAGE 99
R.I.Pie 2018

THE RUBY
SEE PAGE 137
R.I.Pie 2021

CHILLI CON CARNAGE
SEE PAGE 96
R.I.Pie 2018

CHICKEN OF ARAGON

SEE PAGE 37
R.I.Pie 2022

HOLY CHIPOTLE

SEE PAGE 134
R.I.Pie 2022

EVERGREEN

SEE PAGE 38
R.I.Pie 2021

MATADOR

SEE PAGE 102
R.I.Pie 2019

THAI CHOOK

SEE PAGE 136
R.I.Pie 2015

MOO DOG

SEE PAGE 167
R.I.Pie 2020

CROFTER'S PIE

SEE PAGE 109
R.I.Pie 2008

FLOUR POWER!

LOVE YOUR LEF-DOUGH-VERS! OUR PASTRY RECIPES INCLUDE TIPS ON FREEZING, CHILLING AND TURNING YOUR TRIMMINGS INTO TREATS.

PASTRY

PLANT-BASED SUET,
ROUGH PUFF OR SOURDOUGH –
THE PERFECT PASTRIES

PASTRY

The key to making good pastry? Keeping a cool head. Meaning: don't worry about making mistakes. Sometimes you'll find the doughs break a bit when preparing them. This is fine – just patch up any cracks with spare bits of dough. The pie will still look and taste delicious once it's baked. Also, try to keep your hands cool too, so that the fat in the pastry doesn't get too greasy.

When making pastry, often more crumbly means more delicious, BUT it has to be workable and not completely fall apart when you roll it out. In this section, we've included the minimum amount of water needed for each pastry, but you may find you need more. It will depend on the flour you use, the temperature in your kitchen, whether there's an R in the month :-). We know the importance of great pastry, but we also know that it's good to experiment a little and find your own level.

Improvise. Rather than buy a new dish, adapt the shape of your pie to fit into something ovenproof you already have.

We sometimes like to mix the pastries in a pie, combining a shortcrust base and a suet top for example. But it'll still be delicious if you decide to use just one kind.

To get a really crisp pie base, put your pie dish on a hot baking sheet in the oven. Baking blind (when the recipe requires) makes a huge difference too, as does making sure your filling's not too liquid or too hot when added on to the base before baking.

There's no need to use clingfilm when resting your pastry prior to cooking. A clean, damp tea towel over a bowl, reusable food wrap or an airtight container will all do the job just as well.

As a general rule it is better to cook pastry within a couple of hours of making it if you can. That said, most pastries made the night before or defrosted will still be delicious, just not perfect (but perfection's overrated anyway, right?)

Our last tip to avoid the dreaded soggy bottom? Use metal pie dishes and tins.

And make good use of any spare dough. We've added a few suggestions for turning your trimmings into tasty little extras throughout the book.

VEGAN ALMOND & OLIVE OIL PASTRY

This pastry is very short and can be tricky to work with so be prepared to use any trimmings to patch things up. But trust us, it's a cracking recipe (excuse the pun) so well worth the effort. Don't forget to pop the olive oil in the fridge well in advance, for it to solidify!

Makes about 650g (1lb 7oz)

Takes 15 minutes (plus 4 hours for chilling the oil beforehand)

Rest 1 hour

115ml (3¾fl oz) extra virgin olive oil

75g (2¾oz) flaked almonds

300g (10½oz) plain flour, plus extra for dusting

⅔ teaspoon xanthan gum

¼ teaspoon salt

150g (5½oz) icing sugar

2½ tablespoons light demerara sugar

5 tablespoons ice-cold water

1½ teaspoons orange zest

¼ teaspoon almond extract

Chill the olive oil in the fridge for at least 4 hours to allow it to solidify.

Blitz the flaked almonds in a food processor for 20 seconds, or until they form a textured crumb. You can use ground almonds but whizzing flaked almonds leaves a few nice chunky bits.

In a large bowl, mix the almonds, flour, xanthan gum, salt and both sugars together. Add the solidified oil and mix it through with your fingertips until if forms a crumb texture with no large lumps. In a separate bowl, whisk the water, orange zest and almond extract lightly with a fork. Make a well in the centre of the dry ingredients, gently pour in the wet ingredients and mix with a fork to form a crumbly mixture. Turn the pastry out on to a floured work surface and knead with your hands until it just forms a ball of dough, adding a little more water if required.

Transfer the pastry to a bowl and cover with a damp tea towel or wrap in reusable wrap and rest in the fridge for at least 1 hour before use. You can leave the pastry to rest in the fridge for up to a day, stored in an airtight container. It also freezes well.

TOP TIP

MAKE SURE TO USE A VERY GOOD EXTRA VIRGIN OLIVE OIL SO THAT IT WILL SOLIDIFY IN THE FRIDGE.

BROWN BUTTER PASTRY

Incorporating the classic beurre noisette method, this pastry is as brown and nutty as the name suggests. This is a good one to use in the place of the sourdough pastry recipe on page 25 if you're not the sort of person to have a sourdough starter knocking about the kitchen.

Makes about 750g (1lb 10oz)
Takes 30 minutes (plus extra for solidifying the butter)
Rest 30 minutes

250g (9oz) salted butter
500g (1lb 2oz) plain flour, plus extra for dusting
3 tablespoons ice-cold water

Heat the butter in a heavy-based saucepan over a low heat; the butter will first melt, then start to bubble and foam. Swirl the pan a little, but do not stir. The butter will then become clear, and the solids will drop to the bottom of the pan and start to brown. Watch very closely at this stage as it can burn easily. Once the butter solids start to brown and smell nutty after a few minutes, remove the pan from the heat and carefully pour the butter into a heatproof bowl. Chill in the fridge until solid.

When the butter is chilled, chop it up and add it to the flour in a large bowl. Rub the butter into the flour until there are no large lumps left. Mix in the ice-cold water; at this point you should be able to squeeze the dough in your fist and it will stick together. You may need to add a little extra water if not.

Turn the dough out on to a floured work surface and knead for a minute. Transfer the pastry to a bowl and cover with a damp tea towel or wrap in reusable wrap and rest in the fridge for 30 minutes before use.

TOP TIP

IF YOU WOULD LIKE TO USE THE BROWN BUTTER PASTRY FOR A SWEET PIE, STIR IN 2 TABLESPOONS OF CASTER SUGAR BEFORE YOU ADD THE WATER.

SCAN TO WATCH HOW WE MADE THESE RECIPES

PATTY PASTRY

Our version of a Jamaican patty pastry, we get the gorgeous golden colour from saffron, rather than the traditional turmeric. A great plant-based pastry that's super-simple to work with.

Makes 650g (1lb 7oz)
Takes 10 minutes
Rest 30 minutes

⅔ teaspoon saffron strands

130ml (4½fl oz) ice-cold water

380g (13oz) plain flour, plus extra for dusting

3g salt

135g (4¾oz) plant-based or salted butter

Start by adding the saffron to the water. Then, in a large bowl, mix the flour with the salt, and rub in the fat with your fingers until there are no lumps. Make a well in the centre of the flour mix and add the cold saffron water.

Use your hands or a table knife to start mixing the dough and, as it starts to come together, tip it out on to a floured work surface and knead it for a further 2 minutes.

Transfer the pastry to a bowl and cover with a damp tea towel or wrap in reusable wrap and rest in the fridge for 30 minutes before using. You can leave the pastry to rest in the fridge for a few hours and it also freezes well.

SWEET PASTRY

Short and sweet, this is the recipe for tart cases and dessert pies. It's also rather crumbly, but don't despair if it breaks a little while lining a tin with it – just patch it up!

Makes about 700g (1lb 9oz)
Takes 10 minutes
Rest 4 hours+

250g (9oz) unsalted butter, softened
125g (4½oz) icing sugar
1 tablespoon whipping cream
1 free-range egg yolk
350g (12oz) plain flour, plus extra for dusting

Using an electric mixer, cream the butter until light and fluffy. Beat in the icing sugar, then the cream and egg yolk.

Mix in the flour on a slow speed until just combined, then turn out on to a floured work surface and knead lightly for a few seconds until smooth. Transfer the pastry to a bowl and cover with a damp tea towel or wrap in reusable wrap and rest in the fridge for at least 4 hours before use. It will keep in the fridge in an airtight container or wrap for a couple of days and also freezes well.

LEFTOVER RECIPE

SABLÉ BISCUITS

(To use up Sweet or Vegan Almond & Olive Oil pastries)

Press any pastry trimmings together, roll them out to about 5mm (¼in) thick, then cut out whatever shapes you fancy with a pastry cutter. Place on a greased baking sheet, brush with beaten egg or plant-based milk and bake at 180°C/160°C fan/350°F/gas mark 4 for 8–10 minutes until pale golden.

GLUTEN-FREE PASTRY

Gluten-free pastry behaves very differently to regular pastry as the lack of gluten in the flour makes it more like a paste. Keep this in mind when pairing it with a pie tin – you will find it easier to line a shallow metal tin than a deep ceramic dish, for example.

Makes enough for 1 large pie
Takes 10 minutes, plus 30 minutes chilling

500g (1lb 2oz) gluten-free flour
½ teaspoon salt
200g (7oz) butter, diced
300ml (10fl oz) whole milk
1 free-range egg

Put the flour, salt and butter in the bowl of a stand mixer fitted with the dough hook. Mix until the butter is crumbed into the flour. Add the milk and the egg and mix until it forms a thick paste. Chill for 30 minutes before use. This also freezes well.

To line a pie tin with this pastry it can be easier to put a ball of the pastry in the middle of the tin and use greaseproof paper and your fingers to push it out over the base and sides of the pie tin.

To roll the pastry into a pie lid, you may want to do this between floured pieces of greaseproof paper.

Some suggestions for great GF pies:

- Chicken of Aragon (page 37)
- Cheesy Cottage Pie (page 52)
- Dusty Daisy's Knuckle (page 65)
- Mighty Aphrodite (page 99)
- Matador (page 102)
- Minty Lamb (page 154)
- Mooless and Blueless (page 163)

FOODLE PASTRY

This filo x strudel pastry hybrid is a cheat's dream. Much easier to make than traditional filo, which can take years to master, this version is far more forgiving and works just as well for strudels as it does for filo-based treats.

Makes about 650g (1lb 7oz) or 7 sheets
Takes 1 hour
Rest 2 hours

445g strong white bread flour, plus extra for dusting
a generous pinch of salt
170ml (6fl oz) cold water
7 tablespoons olive oil, plus extra for greasing

Put the flour, salt and water in an electric mixer. Attach the dough hook and mix at speed 1 while slowly adding the oil. A dough should form after about 5 minutes. Add a little more water if it's not a nice dough ball at this stage. Continue to knead in the machine for another 10 minutes to develop the gluten. Roll the ball in a little olive oil, place in a bowl and cover with a damp cloth. Rest in a warm place for a couple of hours.

Divide the dough into seven equal-sized pieces, using a dough scraper to shape each piece into a rectangle, and roll to 5mm (¼in) thick on a lightly floured board. Cover with a cloth and allow to rest again for 10 minutes.

Cover your work surface with a smooth, clean tea towel, lightly dust it with flour and place one piece of dough onto it. Putting your hands palms down over the dough at the edges, gently stretch the dough, rotating the tea towel 90 degrees as you go until the dough is stretched as thin as tissue paper and roughly the size of a piece of A4 paper. If it gets the odd little hole in it, this is fine. Use either a pizza cutter or a pair of scissors to trim the edges if they are too thick — you want to avoid too much waste dough here, but if you do end up with a few trimmings, they can be baked with sugar to make lovely little crisps to serve with ice cream!

Repeat with each piece of dough, covering the stretched pieces with a damp cloth while you work on the next. When stacking, dust a little bit of flour between each sheet to avoid them sticking together.

We like to use the foodle pastry straight away; this means being organized and having your fillings at the ready.

1.

2.

3.

4.

5.

6.

7.

8.

9.

10.

 SCAN TO WATCH HOW
WE MADE THESE RECIPES

MIGHTY WHITE PASTRY

We first developed this for a range of topless pies we made a few years back. Inspired by 'that' sliced bread of the same name, this is all about sneaking in some healthy wholemeal flour along with the white.

Makes about 650g (1lb 7oz)
Takes 10 minutes
Rest 30 minutes

255g (9oz) strong white bread flour

130g (4½oz) plain wholemeal flour

½ teaspoon salt

½ teaspoon bicarbonate of soda

125g (4½oz) salted or plant-based butter

100ml (3½fl oz) water

25g (1oz) Parmesan or plant-based hard cheese, finely grated

10g (¼oz) poppy seeds

In a large bowl, mix the flours with the salt and bicarbonate of soda, then rub in the fat with your fingertips until there are no lumps. Make a well in the centre of the flour mix and add the cold water.

Mix and knead the dough and, as it starts to come together, add the Parmesan and poppy seeds. Transfer the pastry to a bowl and cover with a damp tea towel or wrap in reusable wrap and rest in the fridge for 30 minutes before using it. It can be kept in the fridge for a few hours in an airtight container or wrap and freezes well.

FLOUR TIP

This pastry is good for making cold-eating pies, savoury tarts and quiche.

If you'd like to experiment with other flours such as rye or spelt, swap out half of the wholemeal flour. You may need to add a little extra water too. Try this with other seeds as well if you're feeling adventurous.

OLIVE OIL PASTRY

Created especially for our Timpano pies, the olive flavour shines through. Quite simply delicious.

Makes about 300g (10½oz)
Takes 20 minutes
Rest 5 minutes

250g (9oz) plain flour, plus extra for dusting
2 free-range eggs
½ teaspoon salt
2 tablespoons olive oil
3 tablespoons water

Put the flour, eggs, salt and olive oil in the bowl of stand mixer fitted with the dough hook.

Add the water and mix. Add more water, 1 tablespoon at a time, until the mixture comes together to form a ball.

Turn the dough out on to a lightly floured work surface and knead for about 10 minutes to make sure it is well mixed. Rest for 5 minutes before use. If not using immediately, store in the fridge in an airtight container or wrap for up to a day.

GO PLANT BASED

IF YOU WANT TO MAKE THIS VEGAN, YOU CAN REPLACE THE EGGS WITH ½ TEASPOON OF XANTHAN GUM AND INCREASE THE WATER TO 100ML (3½FL OZ).

SOURDOUGH PASTRY

This is yet another great way to put your starter to good use. But if you don't have one, the Brown Butter pastry recipe's a brilliant alternative.

Makes about 650g (1lb 7oz)
Takes 1 hour
Rest 30 minutes

2g citric acid
30ml (1fl oz) cold water
100g (3½oz) plain wholemeal flour
260g strong white bread flour
4g salt
110g (3¾oz) butter or plant-based butter
145g (5oz) sourdough starter or discard, on the wetter side

Dissolve the citric acid in the water.

In a large bowl, mix the flours and salt together and then crumble in the fat. Rub the fat into the flour until it has a sandy texture without any large lumps. Slowly add the water and sourdough starter and mix until it forms a dough. You may need to add more water, depending on the wetness of your starter. Knead a few times in the bowl to form a soft ball, then cover with a damp tea towel or wrap in reusable wrap and rest in the fridge for 30 minutes before use. It will keep in the fridge in an airtight container or wrap for a few hours and also freezes well.

ROUGH PUFF PASTRY

AKA flaky pastry. It still has all the lip-smacking qualities of 'proper' puff pastry but is far easier to make. Just stick to the rules; keep your butter cold and don't over work it – little lumps of butter in the dough is a good thing here.

Makes about 650g (1lb 7oz)
Takes 30 minutes
Rest 1½ hours

250g (9oz) plain flour, plus extra for dusting

a pinch of salt

250g (9oz) cold butter or plant-based butter, cut into 1cm (½in) cubes

150ml (5fl oz) ice-cold water

1 teaspoon lemon juice

Sift the flour into a bowl and add the salt and fat. Mix the water with the lemon juice and add three-quarters of it to the flour mixture. Stir briefly until everything comes together into a rough, shaggy dough. Add the remaining water if necessary.

Turn the dough out on to a floured work surface and press out into a square, then roll out into a long rectangle about 8mm (⅜in) thick. Don't turn the pastry as you roll it but be sure to lift it and flour underneath if it begins to stick.

With the short edge of the pastry closest to you, fold the bottom third up and the top third over that, folding like a business letter. Give it a quarter turn and roll out again. It's best to work quickly so the fat doesn't warm up too much.

Fold in thirds again, wrap in reusable wrap and rest in the fridge for about 20 minutes. Repeat the rolling, folding and chilling twice more, chilling for 20 minutes between each roll and fold, then wrap again and chill for 30 minutes before use. It will keep in the fridge in an airtight container or wrap for up to a day and also freezes well.

LEFTOVER RECIPE

JAM TARTS

(TO USE UP ROUGH PUFF, SHORTCRUST, SWEET AND BROWN BUTTER PASTRIES)

PRESS ANY PASTRY TRIMMINGS TOGETHER, ROLL THEM OUT TO ABOUT 3MM (⅛IN) THICK, THEN CUT OUT ROUNDS WITH A PASTRY CUTTER AND USE TO LINE A BUN TRAY. PUT A LITTLE JAM, LEMON CURD OR MARMALADE IN EACH ONE AND BAKE AT 180°C/160°C FAN/350°F/GAS MARK 4 FOR 6–8 MINUTES UNTIL THE PASTRY EDGES ARE GOLDEN.

SHORTCRUST PASTRY

Our go-to pastry at Pieminister, this is about as versatile as it gets. In our bid to reduce the amount of dairy we use (and make it easier to adapt it for vegan customers), we've switched the milk out for water, and it's every bit as good.

Makes about 650g (1lb 7oz)
Takes 10 minutes
Rest 30 minutes

400g (14oz) plain flour, plus extra for dusting
a pinch of salt
200g (7oz) cold butter or plant-based butter,
    cut into 1cm (½in) cubes
4 tablespoons cold water

Sift the flour into a bowl and add the salt. Drop in the cubes of fat and gently rub them into the flour with your fingertips until the fat is dispersed and the mixture looks like breadcrumbs.

Gradually stir in enough water to make a pliable but fairly firm dough. Turn the dough out on to a floured work surface and knead lightly for 30 seconds until smooth. Transfer the pastry to a bowl and cover with a damp tea towel or wrap in reusable wrap and rest in the fridge for at least 30 minutes before use. It will keep in the fridge in an airtight container or wrap for a couple of hours and also freezes well.

USE IT UP!

CHEESE STRAWS

(TO USE UP SHORTCRUST, ROUGH PUFF OR SUET PASTRIES)

PRESS THE PASTRY TRIMMINGS TOGETHER, ROLL THEM OUT TO ABOUT 3MM (⅛IN) THICK, THEN CUT INTO 5CM (2IN) WIDE STRIPS. BRUSH WITH BEATEN EGG OR A PLANT-BASED MILK AND SCATTER GENEROUSLY WITH DAIRY OR VEGAN CHEESE AND/OR HERBS. BLUE CHEESE AND ROSEMARY IS A PARTICULARLY GOOD COMBO. PLACE ON A GREASED BAKING SHEET AND BAKE AT 180°C/160°C FAN/350°F/GAS MARK 4 FOR 6–8 MINUTES.

SUET PASTRY

This is what we use to achieve the perfect crispy crunch of our pie lids. Steam the recipe rather than bake it and it's a different beast altogether.

Makes about 750g (1lb 10oz)
Takes 10 minutes
Rest 30 minutes

400g (14oz) plain flour, plus extra for dusting
½ teaspoon salt
200g (7oz) vegetable suet
about 120–150ml (4–5fl oz) dairy or
    plant-based milk

Put the flour and salt into a bowl and stir in the suet. Gradually add the milk, adding enough to make a fairly stiff dough. Be sure to add it very slowly or you might find the mixture becomes saturated. If this does happen, add a little extra flour.

Turn the dough out on to a lightly floured surface and knead for a couple of minutes until smooth. You can treat this pastry a little more firmly than ones made with butter.

Transfer the pastry to a bowl and cover with a damp tea towel or wrap in reusable wrap and rest in the fridge for 30 minutes before use. You can leave the pastry to rest in the fridge in an airtight container or wrap for a few hours and it does freeze but is so quick to make it's ideal to use fresh.

OFFCUT RECIPE

SWEET OR SAVOURY TURNOVERS

(USE UP ANY PASTRY — ALSO A GREAT WAY TO USE UP ANY LEFTOVER PIE FILLING)

ROLL OUT THE LEFTOVER PASTRY TO ABOUT 3MM (⅛in) THICK AND CUT OUT CIRCLES 12–15CM (4½–6in) IN DIAMETER. PLACE THE FILLING IN THE MIDDLE OF ONE HALF OF EACH PASTRY CIRCLE, BRUSH THE PASTRY EDGES WITH WATER, THEN FOLD OVER TO COVER THE FILLING. SEAL WELL, CRIMPING HOWEVER YOU LIKE. BRUSH WITH BEATEN EGG OR PLANT-BASED MILK, THEN PLACE ON A BAKING SHEET AND BAKE AT 180°C/160°C FAN/350°F/GAS MARK 4 FOR ABOUT 20 MINUTES UNTIL THE PASTRY IS GOLDEN BROWN AND THE FILLING IS PIPING HOT.

BARKING UP THE WRONG TREE?

CARBON SEQUESTERING, FLOOD ALLEVIATING, BIODIVERSITY PROTECTING, SOIL SUPPORTING... FOREST BATHING?!

Trees do a lot. When we lose them, we set off spiralling climate cycles. We also rob indigenous communities of their homelands.

Just four products are responsible for almost three-quarters of the world's deforestation: beef, soy, palm and paper.

But cutting down what we choose to print in the office will only scratch the surface, as animal rearing is by far the biggest driver of our loss of trees. Beef ranching accounts for 41% and oilseeds, of which soy and palm are the largest, totals 18%. And your soya milk latte isn't really the problem: 77% of the world's soy is fed to animals – mainly chickens and pigs.

PALM OIL

We know there might be an outcry from some of you when we write this but here we go.

Yes, there is such a thing as truly sustainable palm oil.

Read below the 'Boycott Dirty Palm Oil!' headlines and you'll find that Sir David Attenborough, Greenpeace and the World Wildlife Fund are just some of the planet-loving experts telling us that identity preserved (IP) palm oil is the most responsible oil to consume.

Identity preserved palm oil comes from a single certified source kept separately from any other palm oil throughout the supply chain, so that every drop can be traced back to the farm it originates from.

It has a far lower carbon footprint than butter. And it uses less land than other vegetable oils. In fact, palm crops use up to ten times less land than alternatives such as shea and coconut oil for example.

To boycott all palm oil is dangerous; it merely displaces the issue of deforestation and biodiversity loss to these other crops, some of which have no certification schemes at all.

But it is true, palm oil certification schemes have a shady reputation. As consumers, we should demand that brands tell us exactly where their palm oil comes from. If they can show that it is identity preserved (IP), they and the smallholder growers who supply them deserve our support.

A few years ago, we spent a lot of time exploring the most sustainable fats to use in our pastry. Once it became clear that IP palm was the most sustainable choice, we went to Colombia to meet one of the world's most transparent palm oil producers. Their palm oil is grown on land that has never been deforested and is 100% traceable at any given point in the supply chain as it all stays in-house, from the plantations to the refineries and even to the transport (they have their own port!).

But it's no wonder we're not sure which choices to make; the global supply chain is so complex that we're all really disconnected from our food. For example, a few years ago, we were shocked to discover that not all coconut oil is vegan. Why? Because in some places monkeys are chained to trees to harvest the coconuts!

PALM
OIL
2.84T

SUNFLOWER
OIL
0.71T

RAPESEED
OIL
0.61T

SOYBEAN
OIL
0.45T

COCONUT
OIL
0.26T

GROUNDNUT
OIL
0.14T

OLIVE
OIL
0.34T

AS MORE AND MORE OF US BECOME AWARE OF THE
TRUE BIODIVERSITY COSTS OF OUR FOOD AND START
TO MAKE BETTER CHOICES AS INDIVIDUALS, WE REALLY
CAN MAKE A POSITIVE DIFFERENCE. HERE'S HOW:

**DO THE
PIE
THING**

- Buy products made with identity preserved (IP) palm oil, which is the only way to be sure that the palm you're eating is not responsible for deforestation.

- When choosing oils and fats for cooking, choose organic/pasture-fed butter, or go for organically grown oils if you can, as the overuse of fertilizers and pesticides in oilseed production is bad for our waterways, flora and fauna.

- Check where you source your soy products from. If a company is proud of its sourcing credentials, it will openly declare how and where the beans are grown on its website or packaging. Be mindful of the impact of the meat you consume – reduce and/or buy from sources that don't drive deforestation, such as Pasture for Life certified farms in the UK. In some parts of the world masses of forests are being cut down to graze livestock and grow their feed.

ANYTHING SMALLER THAN
CREDIT CARD SIZE CAN'T BE
RECYCLED AS IT FALLS THROUGH
THE GAPS IN THE RECYCLING
MACHINES. SO GATHER ANY
METAL CAPS AND BOTTLE
TOPS IN A CAN AND SQUASH
THE OPENING CLOSED.

SMALL TIN PIES

LITTLE PIES, CANAPIES, TARTS, PIE-ANGLES & OTHER MINI PASTRY BITES

BEEFY COSSACK

The Cossack name roughly translates as 'adventurer', so don't be fooled by the diminutive size of these pies. Yes, they're small but they really pack a punch (and a kick!). Loosely based on a traditional goulash stew, the potato rules here, soaking up the smoky, rich paprika and cinnamon flavours.

½ **portion of shortcrust pastry (page 27)**

½ **portion of suet pastry (page 28)**

1 free-range egg, beaten

plain flour, for dusting

FOR THE FILLING

1 tablespoon organic rapeseed oil, plus extra for greasing

200g (7oz) chuck or stewing steak, cut into 2cm (¾in) dice

1 medium onion, finely diced

3 garlic cloves, crushed

1 carrot, peeled and finely diced

2 teaspoons paprika, plus extra to serve

2 teaspoons ground cinnamon

1 tablespoon tomato purée

2 tablespoons plain flour, plus extra for dusting

150ml (5fl oz) red wine

1 tablespoon red wine vinegar

500ml (18fl oz) beef or vegetable stock

100g (3½oz) potato, peeled and cut into 1cm (½in) dice

100g (3½oz) roasted red peppers, roughly chopped

salt and freshly ground black pepper

TO SERVE

sour cream

chopped chives

Heat the oil in a heavy-based casserole and, when hot, brown the meat on all sides until well caramelized. Reduce the heat to medium–low, add the onion, garlic and carrot to the pan, put on the lid and cook gently for 5 minutes, stirring occasionally.

Sprinkle over the paprika and cinnamon, season well and stir. Stir in the tomato purée, then the flour. Cook for 2–3 minutes, stirring continuously. Increase the heat to medium, slowly add the wine, vinegar, then the stock, stirring constantly, and bring to a simmer. Put on the lid and cook for 1 hour, stirring occasionally, until the meat is very tender.

Add the potatoes and peppers to the pan and check the seasoning. Take off the lid and continue to cook for another 15 minutes. Remove from the heat and leave to cool.

When the filling has cooled, preheat the oven to 180°C/160°C fan/ 350°F/gas mark 4.

Grease one 12-hole bun tin. Dust a work surface with flour and roll out the shortcrust pastry to 3mm (⅛in) thick. Cut 12 circles to line the bun tin and gently press into the holes. Spoon a heaped tablespoon of the cooled filling into each one.

Roll out the suet pastry to 3mm (⅛in) thick and cut 12 slightly smaller lids to fit the pies. Press the edges together to seal the pies, brush with the beaten egg, then leave to stand for 5 minutes before baking for 25 minutes until golden brown.

Serve sprinkled with a little extra paprika and top with a dollop of sour cream and a sprinkle of chopped chives.

JACK YOUR BODY

AS WITH ALL OUR BEEF RECIPES, TRY TO SOURCE THE BEST BEEF YOU CAN TO MINIMIZE THE ENVIRONMENTAL IMPACT. READ MORE ON PAGE 117.

JACKFRUIT IS A GREAT PLANT-BASED REPLACEMENT FOR THE BEEF IN THIS RECIPE. USE 1 PORTION OF THE JACKFRUIT RECIPE ON PAGE 180.

CHICKEN OF ARAGON

Divorced, beheaded, died. Divorced, beheaded, survived... Like this recipe's namesake, this pie once ruled the Pieminister range, until The Freeranger Pie™ arrived on the scene and stole her crown. Now, with this recipe, you can reinstate her. Long live the Queen!

½ **portion of shortcrust pastry (page 27)**

½ **portion of suet pastry (page 28)**

1 free-range egg, beaten

plain flour, for dusting

FOR THE FILLING

1 tablespoon organic rapeseed oil

4 rashers of free-range smoked streaky bacon, finely sliced

1 small onion, finely diced

2 garlic cloves, crushed

1 small leek, washed, halved and finely sliced

350g (12oz) free-range chicken thigh fillets, cut into 2cm (¾in) dice

¼ celeriac (150–200g/5½–7oz), peeled and cut into 1cm (½in) dice

125ml (4fl oz) white vermouth

200ml (7fl oz) chicken stock

1 tablespoon Dijon mustard

3 sprigs of thyme

1 bay leaf

1 teaspoon cornflour

50ml (2fl oz) double cream

10 sprigs of tarragon, leaves picked and finely chopped

salt and freshly ground black pepper

Heat the oil in a heavy-based casserole dish over a medium heat and, when hot, add the sliced bacon to the pan and cook gently until the fat has rendered out of the bacon. Add the onion, garlic and leeks, season with salt and pepper, put on the lid and cook gently for 10 minutes, stirring occasionally.

Turn up the heat to medium-high, add the diced chicken and celeriac to the pan, and stir. Add the vermouth and cook for 2–3 minutes to reduce, stirring continuously. Reduce the heat to medium, add the stock, Dijon mustard, thyme and bay leaf and bring to a simmer. Put on the lid and cook for 40 minutes–1 hour, stirring occasionally, until the meat and celeriac are tender but not falling apart.

Dissolve the cornflour in 1 tablespoon of warm water and add to the mix, stirring continuously to thicken the mixture. Cook for a further 5 minutes. Add the double cream and the tarragon to the pan, check the seasoning and allow to heat through. Remove from the heat and leave to cool, discarding the bay leaf and thyme stalks.

When the filling has cooled, preheat the oven to 180°C/160°C fan/ 350°F/gas mark 4. Dust a work surface with flour and roll out the shortcrust pastry to 3mm (⅛in) thick. Cut circles to line a 12-hole bun tin (or 24 smaller circles if doing canapies in a mini-bun tin) and gently press into the holes. Spoon 1 tablespoon of cooled filling into each one.

Roll out the suet pastry to 3mm (⅛in) thick and cut 12 (or 24) slightly smaller lids to fit the pies. Press the edges together to seal the pies and brush with the beaten egg. Leave to stand for 5 minutes, then bake for 15–20 minutes until golden brown.

THERE ARE SO MANY DIFFERENT LABELS ON PORK OUT THERE IT CAN GET VERY CONFUSING, CAN'T IT?! ONES SUCH AS 'RED TRACTOR', 'OUTDOOR-REARED' OR 'OUTDOOR-BRED' AREN'T AS HIGH WELFARE AS THEY'D LIKE YOU TO BELIEVE. WE RECOMMEND LOOKING OUT FOR 'FREE RANGE' OR EVEN 'ORGANIC' TO MAKE SURE YOU'RE SUPPORTING HIGH-WELFARE PORK FARMERS.

EVERGREEN FILO TRIANGLES

Green by name and green by nature, this lush and verdant recipe won a whopping three gold stars in 'The Oscars of the food world'. The flagship pie for our Eat Pies: Plant Trees campaign, it helped us plant a new forest in Kent with Forestry England. A handful of these makes a great plant-based main served with a salad or two. Or hand them around at a party, served with tahini dipping sauce.

7 sheets of ready-rolled filo pastry

olive oil, for brushing

FOR THE FILLING

½ small courgette (or about 90g/3¼oz)

2 garlic cloves, finely chopped

4cm (1½in) piece of fresh ginger, peeled and finely chopped

1 spring onion, finely chopped

120g (4¼oz) frozen edamame beans, defrosted

50g (1¾oz) baby leaf spinach

50g (1¾oz) curly kale, hard stalks removed

70g (2½oz) broccoli, broken into small florets

a small handful of chopped fresh coriander

a small handful of chopped fresh mint

zest and juice of 1 lime

¼ teaspoon bicarbonate of soda

salt and freshly ground black pepper

nigella seeds, to garnish

FOR THE TAHINI & MINT DIP

4 tablespoons tahini paste

2 garlic cloves, crushed with salt

3 tablespoons extra virgin olive oil, plus extra to serve

juice of 1 lime

about 4 tablespoons cold water

chopped fresh mint, to taste

Preheat the oven to 200°C/180°C fan/400°F/gas mark 6 and line a baking tray with baking parchment.

Grate the courgette into a bowl and add the garlic, ginger and spring onion. Add the defrosted edamame beans.

Finely chop the baby leaf spinach and curly kale and tumble together with the courgette mixture and the broccoli, coriander, mint and lime zest. Mix well.

In a small bowl, combine the lime juice and bicarbonate of soda – it will fizz up a bit. Pour this mixture over the green veg – the combination of the citric acid and the sodium bicarbonate prevents pH changes, and helps to retain the lovely green colour of the veg.

Lay the filo pastry sheets on to a work surface and cut each pastry sheet into 4 long strips horizontally. Take one strip and cover the rest of the filo with a damp tea towel until needed, to stop it drying out. Place a tablespoon of the filling on the bottom left side of the strip. Fold the bottom right corner up over it, in a triangle. Fold that triangle up then continue folding in a triangular fashion until the whole strip is used. Place on the lined baking tray and repeat with the remaining pastry strips and filling.

Brush the pastry triangles with olive oil and sprinkle with the nigella seeds. Bake for 12–15 minutes.

Meanwhile, to make the tahini and mint dip, blend the tahini, garlic, olive oil and lime juice together in a food processor or blender, then add enough cold water to make a smooth sauce. Stir in the chopped mint. Place in the fridge to chill and drizzle with a little olive oil just before serving.

Serve the evergreen triangles hot or cold with the tahini dipping sauce.

WASTE NOT WANT NOT!

Did you know that you can magically grow a new spring onion from an old one? Put a chopped-off bulb in a small jar with enough water to cover the roots, and the top edges sticking out of the water. Leave on a windowsill and green shoots will emerge after a few days. Change the water every week and keep snipping off what you need, the spring onion will continue growing!

FETA HONEY BITES

Our Head Chef, Matt 'Sparkles' Sparkes came up with this insanely good pastry. Somewhere between filo and strudel pastry, it's the ideal foil to the spiced honeyed cheese. Moreish. You can make these little crunchy bombs of cheesy goodness with pre-made filo, but we highly recommend you make your own if you have the time and inclination – trust us, it's worth the effort!

4 sheets filo or foodle pastry (page 22)

FOR THE FILLING

½ teaspoon cumin seeds

80g (2¾oz) unsalted butter

1 teaspoon mint jelly

200g (7oz) feta

2 tablespoons local honey

80g (2¾oz) marinated sun-dried peppers in olive oil, drained (drained weight), roughly chopped

a generous grinding of black pepper

a pinch of chilli flakes

FOR THE HARISSA YOGURT

150g (5½oz) Greek yogurt

1 teaspoon harissa

1 tablespoon lemon juice

salt, to taste

Heat a pan over a medium heat and dry-fry the cumin seeds until lightly toasted and fragrant. Leave to cool.

Preheat the oven to 200°C/180°C fan/400°F/gas mark 6 and line a baking tray with baking parchment.

Melt the butter in a heatproof bowl in the microwave and stir in the mint jelly. Set aside.

Using your hands, crumble the feta into a bowl. Add the honey, cooled cumin seeds, sun-dried peppers and black pepper, to taste.

Take one sheet of pastry and lay it out on the work surface. Make sure that the remaining pastry is covered with a damp tea towel to stop it drying out.

Cut each sheet into three pieces lengthways and then cut each in half horizontally, so that you have six smaller sheets. Brush each little filo sheet with the flavoured butter and put a teaspoon of the feta mixture on the top of each sheet.

Fold some of the pastry over the filling, then fold in the edges to stop any filling escaping from either end. Roll each bite into a rectangular mini cigar-like shape and place on the lined baking tray. Brush the top with the mint-flavoured butter – keep stirring the butter to make sure that the mint is distributed equally throughout it. Bake in the oven for 8 minutes.

Remove from the oven, glaze with the butter mixture again, sprinkle over some chilli flakes and return to the oven for about another 5 minutes, or until golden brown and cooked through. Serve hot or cold, but best hot.

For the harissa yogurt, mix together all the ingredients in a small bowl.

LOOK FOR A GOOD-QUALITY LOCAL HONEY FOR THIS RECIPE. WE USED SOMERSET BLOSSOM HONEY – THE WEST COUNTRY HONEY FOLK HAVE A STALL RIGHT NEXT DOOR TO OUR SPOT AT THE TOBACCO FACTORY MARKET IN BRISTOL ON A SUNDAY.

SCARLET ELF CUPS ANYONE?

FiNDiNG FOOD ON yOUR DOORSTEP

Eliza Reid runs a veg box scheme with a difference. She gathers her own-grown produce along with that from local allotment holders and other small-scale growers – even locals with a fruit tree in their garden – along with things she's foraged. Basically, if it's locally grown without the use of chemicals or it's certified organic, Eliza's interested.

So, as well as a weekly bunch of flowers, the lucky recipients of her baskets will find things they've probably never thought to eat. From sea kale and magnolia flowers (a bit like chicory!) to scarlet elf cups and pig nuts, her foraging calendar reads like a shopping list for a magic spell.

The very definition of a circular economy, Eliza also collects any food donations customers leave in their empty baskets to take to local vulnerable families she's got to know, along with any surplus wonky veg she's collected from her growers.

We joined Eliza on a foraging expedition to Lyme Regis for dulse seaweed. Clambering over the weedy rocks at low tide, she showed us how to select the brownest dulse, not the stuff that's been bleached by the sun. And the importance of only picking what you need, taking care to trim a little per plant, leaving the roots intact so that the plant can regenerate.

The properties that make weeds, weeds (hardy, pest resistant, able to grow pretty much anywhere) make them super-foods for humans.

Eliza explained that because they contain ridiculously high levels of vitamins and minerals, they can taste bitter (which most modern palates are unaccustomed to). But bitter is good – it means less sugar – so perhaps it's time we retrain our tastebuds to embrace a bit of tartness.

Here are a few tips to get you started on your sustainable foraging journey:

- Start simply and safely, collecting common plants you can easily identify. Chances are you won't need to go further than your garden or local park. In the UK, we're talking blackberries, crab apples, dandelion leaves, nettle tops, wild garlic and sea kale…the list goes on.

- Only take what you need. Remember, these plants pack a punch in terms of flavour and nutrition, so you really don't need much.

- Never take a whole plant, in fact leave at least half of it to ensure it can grow back for others to enjoy.

NOS DA, CARIAD TARTS

The title translates as 'Good Night, Love' and this does make a deliciously simple supper. But to avoid the risk of cheesy Welsh Rarebit dreams, we recommend leaving a little digestion time before bed. Our friend Alison, who inspired this recipe, grew up eating this in The Valleys, with spring onions to dip into the oozing cheese and tomatoes on the side. We topped this off with some of the dulse seaweed we foraged with Eliza (turn back overleaf) which genuinely tastes like crisp smoky bacon when fried (it really does!). Fry it in a light oil such as organic rapeseed and it takes less than 30 seconds each side (see more in the Tip).

½ **portion of shortcrust pastry (page 27)**

FOR THE FILLING

50g (1¾oz) salted butter

50g (1¾oz) plain flour, plus extra for dusting

300ml (10fl oz) milk

a few gratings of nutmeg

1 teaspoon English mustard

170g (6oz) Caerphilly cheese, such as Gorwydd, crumbled

100ml (3½fl oz) dark Welsh bitter

16 oak-smoked, Isle of Wight sun-blushed tomatoes or regular sun-blushed tomatoes, chopped

a small bunch of chives, chopped

a sprinkle of foraged seaweed, to serve

Dust a work surface with flour, roll out the pastry to 3mm (⅛in) thick and cut to fit 8 individual tart tins; we used 10cm (4in) square tins but 10cm (4in) circular ones will work just as well. Prick the bases with a fork and set aside to rest in the fridge for 30 minutes.

Preheat the oven to 180°C/160°C fan/350°F/gas mark 4.

Put the tart tins on to a baking sheet, line each tart with greaseproof paper, fill it with baking beans or rice and blind bake for 15 minutes until golden and dry. Set aside.

While the pastry is cooking, make the filling. Melt the butter in a saucepan and, when it's foaming, add the flour and cook over a medium heat, stirring continuously, for 3–4 minutes.

Slowly add the milk, stirring after each addition. It may look lumpy at first but keep beating with a wooden spoon or whisk and it will become smooth. Once all the milk is added, keep stirring as it comes to a simmer.

Add the nutmeg, mustard, 150g (5½oz) of the cheese and the bitter, season and stir until everything is incorporated and the sauce is thick.

Divide the tomatoes and chives between the tart cases and spoon in the sauce. Crumble over the remaining cheese and return to the oven for 25–30 minutes until the tarts are golden and bubbling. Leave to cool for a few minutes before serving.

To prepare your seaweed, rinse in fresh water, pat dry (or use a salad spinner) then peg it on a washing line or spread on tea towels on a sunny window sill, it will take up to 2 days to dry. Otherwise lay it on baking sheets in a low oven for approximately 1 hour. It will keep for a year in an airtight container.

WALNUT CANAPIES

How did the Walnut know where the Cashew was hiding? Because he was Pecan!
The Walnut Whip™ first wowed chocolate aficionados in Edinburgh back in 1910.
Here's something else delicious and fun you can do with those crazy little nuts
and a bit of whipping.

375g (13½oz) packet of shop-bought puff pastry
1 free-range egg, beaten
plain flour, for dusting

FOR THE FILLING

12 walnut halves

50g (1¾oz) unsalted butter

2 tablespoons soft brown sugar

6 small red onions, peeled and sliced in half from root to tip

3 sprigs of thyme, leaves picked

1 tablespoon red wine vinegar

100g (3½oz) soft blue cheese, such as Gorgonzola or Roquefort

50g (1¾oz) cream cheese or mascarpone

Preheat the oven to 200°C/180°C fan/400°F/gas mark 6.

Place the walnut halves on a baking sheet and roast in the oven for 5–7 minutes until lightly roasted, watching carefully to ensure that they don't burn. Once roasted, remove from the oven and set aside.

Place a frying pan over a medium heat, add the butter and sugar to the pan and heat gently until melted together and beginning to caramelize. Carefully place the onions cut-side down into the pan. Sprinkle over the thyme leaves and red wine vinegar.

Make a cartouche by cutting a circle of baking parchment slightly larger than your frying pan and lightly pressing it down on the surface of the onions. Allow the onions to cook for 8–10 minutes until just tender when pierced with the tip of a knife. Remove the cartouche and increase the heat to medium–high to reduce any liquid in the pan and lightly caramelize the cut surface of the onions. Remove from the heat and leave to cool.

Dust a work surface with flour and roll out the pastry until 3mm (⅛in) thick. Cut out circles the same size as the holes of a 12-hole bun tin. Place one onion half, cut-side down, into each hole and add 1 teaspoon of liquid from the pan. Take a circle of pastry and place over each onion half, tucking the edges in and around the onion. Prick the surface of each pie with a fork and brush with the beaten egg. Bake in the oven for 15–20 minutes until golden brown.

Meanwhile, mix the blue cheese and cream cheese together – this can be whipped together in a mini food processor or mashed together with a fork.

Remove the pies from the oven, run a small sharp knife or small palette knife around the edge and underneath each pie. Take a board slightly larger than your bun tin and place over the top and, using a tea towel, quickly flip the tin so that the board is underneath and your pies are now on the board onions-side up. If any onions stick to the tin, just remove gently with a teaspoon and place into the pastry case.

Garnish each pie by spooning or piping a generous teaspoon of your whipped blue cheese mixture on to the top of each pie and adding a toasted walnut.

TOP TIP

WALNUTS ARE LITTLE BALLS OF HEALTH! THEY REDUCE BLOOD PRESSURE AND IMPROVE CIRCULATION AND MUSCLE FUNCTION. GO ON, CRACK OPEN ANOTHER...

WILD MUSHROOM VOL AU VENTS

Who doesn't love a vol-au-vent?! Once the height of sophistication, these 70s dinner party classics are making a comeback. French for 'windblown' due to the lightness of the pastry, they're the perfect little pastry pots for this rich, earthy filling, topped with melting West Country clotted cream. Use whichever mushrooms are in season – morels in the spring, portobellos in the winter – or play around with a combo of dried 'shrooms mixed with fresh.

320g (11½oz) ready-rolled puff pastry

1 free-range egg, lightly beaten

plain flour, for dusting

FOR THE FILLING

2 tablespoons olive oil

a knob of butter

1 sprig of thyme

1 large shallot, diced

300g (10½oz) mixed wild or button mushrooms, wiped clean and roughly chopped (smaller mushrooms can be left whole)

1 tablespoon Cognac

1 garlic clove, finely chopped

1 tablespoon finely chopped oregano

1 teaspoon wholegrain mustard

75g (2¾oz) clotted cream

½ teaspoon clear honey (local is always best)

salt and freshly ground black pepper

Preheat the oven to 220°C/200°C fan/425°F/gas mark 7 and line a baking tray with baking parchment.

Dust a work surface with flour and lay out the pastry on the floured surface. Cut out 20 circles using a 6cm (2½in) plain cutter. Using a 4.5cm (1¾in) cutter, cut a smaller circle out of the centre of ten of the circles. Place the ten larger circles on to the baking tray and brush the top of the pastry (but not the sides) with a little of the beaten egg. Place the circles with a hole cut out on top of each of the large circles, leaving an outer ring. (The smaller cut-out circles can be set aside, covered, in the fridge to make another recipe – see the tip below.) Carefully brush the top of the rounds with beaten egg and bake for 10–15 minutes, or until risen and golden brown. Cool on a wire rack.

While the pastry is cooking, prepare the mushroom mixture. Heat 1 tablespoon of the oil and the butter in a frying pan over a medium heat, then add the thyme and shallot and cook for a few minutes, or until softened. Tip in most of the mushrooms (reserving a few of the prettiest mushrooms for garnish) and the remaining tablespoon of oil and cook until the mushrooms are coloured all over, stirring constantly. Add the Cognac and cook to allow the liquid to be absorbed.

Reduce the heat and add the garlic and three-quarters of the oregano, then stir in the wholegrain mustard. Add salt and pepper, to taste, to the mushrooms.

Push down the centre of each vol au vent, fill with the mushroom mixture, top each with a small spoonful of clotted cream, garnish with the remaining oregano and drizzle with honey. Garnish with the reserved mushrooms. Serve at once.

WASTE NOT WANT NOT!

MAKE SOME LOVELY QUICK CHEESY BISCUITS WITH THE PASTRY OFFCUTS FROM THIS RECIPE. SIMPLY GRATE A LITTLE PARMESAN (OR CHEDDAR) OVER THE PASTRY CIRCLES, PLACE ON A BAKING TRAY, BRUSH WITH THE REMAINING BEATEN EGG, AND BAKE IN THE OVEN ONCE THE VOL AU VENTS ARE NEARLY DONE. YOU DON'T WANT TO OPEN THE OVEN DURING THE FIRST THREE-QUARTERS OF THE BAKE (THE PUFF MIGHT DE-PUFF), BUT THESE CHEESY BISCUITS WILL ONLY TAKE ABOUT 5–10 MINUTES, SO MAKE USE OF THE HOT OVEN.

CHEESY COTTAGE PIE PIE

Cottage pie... in a pie! If you can't make up your mind whether to have a pastry or potato pie, why not plump for both? We've cooked the mince with our fruity brown sauce to give it an extra umami kick and topped it off with some creamy cheesy mash.

½ **portion of shortcrust pastry (page 27)**

1 free-range egg, beaten

plain flour, for dusting

FOR THE FILLING

2 teaspoons olive oil, plus extra for greasing

1 large onion, diced

500g (1lb 2oz) beef mince

½ teaspoon dried thyme

1 teaspoon salt

½ teaspoon freshly ground black pepper

2 garlic cloves, finely chopped

1 tablespoon tomato purée

1 bay leaf

350ml (12fl oz) beef stock

3 tablespoons fruity brown sauce (page 179), plus extra to serve

FOR THE MASH TOPPING

500g (1lb 2oz) floury potatoes, washed and cut into chunks

50g (1¾oz) salted butter, plus extra for greasing

a splash of milk

100g (3½oz) Westcombe Cheddar, finely grated

freshly grated nutmeg

salt and freshly ground black pepper

To make the mince filling, heat the olive oil in a pan, add the onion and fry until softened. Crumble the beef into the pan and cook, breaking up the meat with a wooden spoon. Add the thyme, salt and black pepper. Once the meat has browned all over, add the garlic and stir to combine, then stir in the tomato purée.

Add the bay leaf and beef stock and cook over a low heat for about 1 hour, or until the liquid has thickened and mostly been absorbed by the mince. Stir in the fruity brown sauce about 10 minutes before the end of the cooking time. Remove the bay leaf and discard.

For the mash topping, boil the potatoes in a pan of salted water until cooked (about 15–20 minutes, depending on size). Drain off all the water and replace the lid. Shake the pan, which will start to break up the potatoes. Add the butter and milk, a little at a time, at the same time as mashing the potatoes. Leave to cool. Stir in half of the Cheddar. Season with salt and pepper, to taste.

Preheat the oven to 200°C/180°C fan/400°F/gas mark 6.

Grease two 20cm (8in) pie dishes with oil and butter. Dust a work surface with flour and roll out the pastry to about 3mm (⅛in) thick, then use it to line the pie dishes, trimming off the excess. Use your fingers to crimp the edges of each pie. Place in the fridge for at least 20 minutes.

Brush the inside of the pies with beaten egg and fill with half of the filling. Top with the mashed potatoes – if you are feeling fancy, you could pipe it on – then sprinkle over the remaining cheese and grate over a little nutmeg.

Bake the pies in the oven for 30–35 minutes, or until golden brown. Serve hot or cold with more fruity brown sauce on the side.

FARM FACT

IF YOU CAN, WHEN BUYING YOUR MEAT CHOOSE HIGH-WELFARE, GRASS-FED BEEF, IDEALLY FROM A FARM WITH REGENERATIVE PRACTICES — GO TO PAGE 157 TO READ MORE ABOUT SUSTAINABLE FARMING.

PUMPKIN & PISTACHIO MINI PATTIES

Sweet little buttery, nutty, sticky treats with hints of the Middle East.
Perfect for afternoon teas and picnics, washed down with a cup of tea.

½ **portion of patty pastry (page 20)**

1 free-range egg, beaten

plain flour, for dusting

FOR THE FILLING

3 tablespoons runny honey (local is always best)

1 teaspoon ground cinnamon

130g (4½oz) unsalted butter

300g (10½oz) pumpkin or butternut squash, peeled and cut into 1cm (½in) cubes

120g (4¼oz) caster sugar

3 free-range eggs

1 tablespoon orange blossom water

60g (2¼oz) ground almonds

200g (7oz) shelled pistachios, blitzed in a blender to the same texture as the almonds

2 tablespoons pistachios, chopped

salt

crème fraîche swirled with orange zest, to serve

Preheat the oven to 200°C/180°C fan/400°F/gas mark 6.
Line a baking tray with baking parchment.

Gently heat 1 tablespoon of the honey with the cinnamon and 10g (¼oz) of the butter. Toss the pumpkin pieces in the mixture and spread on to an oven tray. Sprinkle with a little salt and roast for 15 minutes until browning at the edges. Set aside to cool. Increase the oven temperature to 220°C/200°C fan/425°F/gas mark 7.

Meanwhile, make the frangipane. Whisk the remaining butter and the sugar together in a large bowl until light and fluffy. Beat in two of the eggs, then gently fold in the orange blossom water, almonds and blitzed pistachios to create a smooth batter.

Dust a work surface with flour and roll out the patty pastry to 3mm (⅛in) thick. Cut out eight circles about 12–15cm (4½–6in) wide; we used a side plate to cut around.

Stir the cooled pumpkin into the frangipane. Spoon the pumpkin mixture on to the bottom half of each pastry circle, leaving a 2cm (¾in) border clear around the edge. Brush the edge with the beaten egg, then fold the top half over and press the edges together with a fork, making sure it's completely sealed.

Put the patties on the prepared tray and brush the tops with beaten egg. Let them rest for 5 minutes, then bake for 20 minutes until golden brown.

Mix together the chopped pistachios and the remaining 2 tablespoons of honey. When the patties are cooked, brush them with the honey mixture. Serve with crème fraîche swirled with orange zest.

PEAS & LOVE

PUMPKINS ARE PACKED WITH BETA-CAROTENE, WHICH IS A FREE-RADICAL-FIGHTING ANTI-OXIDANT AND WHAT GIVES PUMPKINS THEIR ORANGE COLOUR.

BOUGIE BAKEWELLS

We've given the dear old Bakewell tart a bit of a makeover and the result?
Glammy, jammy gorgeousness. You can buy ready-made boozy cherries
but, if you make your own, they take at least 4 weeks to mature.

½ **portion of sweet pastry
(page 21)**
plain flour, for dusting

FOR THE FILLING

120g (4¼oz) **unsalted butter**
120g (4¼oz) **caster sugar**
2 **free-range eggs**
1 teaspoon **almond extract**
120g (4¼oz) **ground almonds**
5 heaped tablespoons **icing
sugar**

FOR THE BOOZY CHERRIES

300g (10½oz) **cherries**
zest of 1 **orange**
2–3 sprigs of **thyme**
200g (7oz) **caster sugar**
400ml (14fl oz) **vodka**

To make the boozy cherries, remove the stalks and stones from the cherries and put them into a 1-litre (1¾-pint) sterilized jar. Intersperse the cherries with the orange zest and thyme sprigs. Pour in the sugar and vodka, making sure that the cherries are completely submerged. Shake the jar, then leave in a dark cupboard for a minimum of 4 weeks but ideally 6 weeks, giving it a turn and shake every week or so.

To make the tarts, first convert the boozy cherries into jam. Reserve 12 boozy cherries to decorate the finished tarts and put the remainder into a heavy-based saucepan with 400ml (14fl oz) of the flavoured vodka. Bring to the boil and simmer for a further 15–20 minutes until the liquid becomes thick and jammy. The jam will solidify more as it cools, so don't overcook at this point. Set aside.

Preheat the oven to 190°C/170°C fan/375°F/gas mark 5. Dust a work surface with flour and roll out the pastry to 3cm (1¼in) thick. Use a 9cm (3½in) pastry cutter to cut 12 discs, place them into the holes of a muffin tin and chill in the fridge for 10 minutes. You may need to gather up the trimmings and re-roll to get 12 pastry rounds.

When chilled, place a paper cake case inside each tart, fill with baking beans or rice and blind bake for 15 minutes until golden and dry. Set aside.

Next, make the frangipane. Whisk the butter and caster sugar together in a large bowl until light and fluffy. Beat in the eggs and almond extract, then gently fold in the ground almonds to create a smooth batter.

Spoon 3–4 cooked cherries into each pastry case along with some of the jammy liquid, then top with the frangipane batter. Bake in the oven for 15–20 minutes until golden. Cool on a wire rack.

When the tarts are cool, mix the icing sugar with 1–2 teaspoons of water to make a thickish paste. Spread the icing over the tarts and top each with a reserved cherry. These will keep for 3–4 days in an airtight container.

MOOK DONGLES LAVA PIES

We all love to discover something. Apparently, there's this restaurant that produces some wonderful deep-fried apple pies? Here's our version. Watch out, they're hotter than the sun.

½ **portion of rough puff pastry (page 26) or 500g (1lb 2oz) shop-bought puff pastry**

1 **free-range egg, beaten**

plain flour, for dusting

500ml (18fl oz) **vegetable or sunflower oil**

FOR THE FILLING

6 Granny Smith apples, peeled, cored and cut into 5mm (¼in) dice

20g (¾oz) granulated sugar

20g (¾oz) soft light brown sugar

1 tablespoon syrup from the jar of preserved ginger

¼ teaspoon fine sea salt

½ teaspoon ground cinnamon

25g (1oz) butter or plant-based butter

juice of ½ lemon

½ teaspoon cornflour

1 tablespoon warm water

1 ball of preserved ginger, finely diced

To SERVE

50g (1¾oz) granulated sugar

½ teaspoon ground cinnamon

Place a small saucepan over a medium heat and add the apples, both sugars, preserved ginger syrup, salt, cinnamon, butter and lemon juice. Cook for 5–10 minutes, stirring often, until the sugars have dissolved. Dissolve the cornflour in the warm water and add to the apple mix along with the diced preserved ginger, increase the heat to high and simmer for 5–10 minutes until the mixture has thickened. Remove from the heat and allow the apple mix to cool completely. Place in the fridge until ready to assemble your pies. You can speed up this process by spreading the mixture thinly over a baking sheet and placing in the fridge or freezer.

Dust a work surface with flour and roll out the rough puff pastry to 3mm (⅛in) thick. Then cut it into six rectangles measuring 12 x 16cm (4½ x 6¼in). Cover a baking tray with baking parchment and lightly dust it with flour. Place the pastry rectangles on the baking tray and use a pastry brush dipped in water to paint a 1cm (½in) border around each one. Spoon 3 tablespoons of the apple mix on to the bottom half of each rectangle, avoiding the edges. Fold over the top half of the pastry to form a long rectangle, then shape the pastry around the apple filling to ensure you remove any excess air. Take a fork and dip it in the remaining flour on the tray and use this to seal the edges of the pastry. Repeat for the six pies. Place the pies in the fridge to chill for 1 hour or in the freezer for 20 minutes.

In a shallow bowl, combine the granulated sugar and cinnamon. Line a baking tin with kitchen paper to drain the fried pies.

Take a large, heavy-based saucepan and add the oil. Heat to 190°C (375°F). Remove the chilled pies from the fridge and gently lower each pie into the heated oil using a slotted spoon or spider. Fry the pies individually or two at a time, depending on the size of your pan, for 4–5 minutes, flipping over halfway through cooking. Once golden brown, remove the pies from the oil and drain briefly on the prepared kitchen paper and then toss in the bowl of cinnamon sugar. Remove to a rack to cool slightly before serving.

GRANNY SMITH APPLES GIVE A FANTASTIC TANG, BUT THIS RECIPE COULD ALSO WORK WITH THAT BAG OF HOME-GROWN APPLES GIFTED TO YOU EACH AUTUMN BY ABSOLUTELY EVERYONE WHO HAS AN APPLE TREE IN THEIR GARDEN...

MOTHERSHIP

SUNDAY BEST

MOTHER EARTH

IT'S ALL GRAVY

MORNING GLORY

MAKE A MEAL OF IT

HOW DO YOU LIKE YOURS?

We like to think of our restaurants as a haven for pie lovers, somewhere where their every pie need is met.

Want a pie for breakfast? Done. Want two pies perched precariously on top of each other, on top of a pile of mash and mushy peas? No problemo. Like your pie served with a never-ending supply of gravy? We hear you. Don't like your gravy to touch your pie? We gotcha.

These combos have become so popular, we've given them names, but the list is by no means exhaustive. After all, the pie's the limit.

TOWER OF POWER

GIVE AN OLD DISH A HOME.
RATHER THAN BUY NEW
BAKEWARE, HUNT FOR TREASURE
IN LOCAL CHARITY SHOPS —
THAT'S WHERE WE FOUND MUCH
OF THE STUFF FOR THIS BOOK.

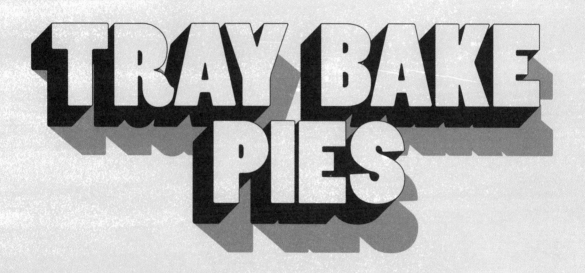

TRAY BAKE PIES

TRAY BAKES, SLICES, FILOS, FLAPJACKS & OTHER SHAREY BAKES

DUSTY DAISY'S KNUCKLE PIE

Many people discovered Pieminister at festivals, and in the early days 19-year-old Daisy ran the show for us – and she smashed it. It is of little surprise that she went on to teach herself to bake, before establishing Dusty Knuckle, one of London's best (and definitely coolest) bakeries... This is Daisy's idea of a carb-on-carb cheese party for the mouth!

1 portion of rough puff pastry (page 26)

plain flour, for dusting

FOR THE FILLING

200g (7oz) sun-blush tomatoes in oil

1 garlic clove

1 tablespoon oregano leaves

1 teaspoon brown sugar

150g (5½oz) smoked Kashkaval cheese, sliced

150g (5½oz) waxy potatoes, thinly sliced

1 tablespoon chopped rosemary

2 teaspoons chipotle chilli flakes

salt and freshly ground black pepper

Line a baking tray with baking parchment. Dust a work surface with flour and roll out the pastry to fit inside the lined baking tray, so it measures about 20 x 30cm (8 x 12in). Leave it to rest while you make the sauce.

Preheat the oven to 180°C/160°C fan/350°F/gas mark 4.

In a blender, blitz the tomatoes, garlic, oregano and sugar. Add 75ml (2½fl oz) of the oil from the tomato jar and blend to a smooth-ish paste. Season well. Spread the tomato paste over the pastry, then top with slices of cheese and the potatoes. Scatter with the rosemary and drizzle with a little oil from the tomato jar.

Bake for 20 minutes and serve sprinkled with the chilli flakes.

DAISY'S YOUTH PROGRAMME AT THE BAKERY HELPS YOUNG PEOPLE AT RISK OF LONG-TERM CRIMINALITY AND UNEMPLOYMENT WITH ON-THE-JOB TRAINING AND MENTORING. THERE ARE PURPOSE-DRIVEN FOOD BUSINESSES LIKE THIS EVERYWHERE AND WE CAN SUPPORT THEM BY EATING THEIR DELICIOUS GOODS. WIN-WIN!

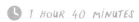

DEEP PAN PIZZA PIE

Deep sides mean more filling. Which is why we'll always plump for pies over pizzas. But clever Chicago had the right idea when they engineered their deep pan pizza tins and created the pizza pie! Wish we'd thought of that first...

2 portions of olive oil pastry (page 25)

FOR THE FILLING

400g (14oz) mozzarella, cut into thin slices

50g (1¾oz) Parmesan, grated

40g (1½oz) 'nduja

basil leaves, to serve

FOR THE SAUCE

1 tablespoon olive oil

1 onion, finely diced

600g (1lb 5oz) ripe tomatoes, chopped

1 tablespoon tomato purée

1 tablespoon balsamic vinegar

2 garlic cloves, crushed

1 tablespoon oregano leaves

1 teaspoon chilli flakes

½ teaspoon sugar

salt and freshly ground black pepper

To make the sauce, heat the oil in a large, heavy-based saucepan and gently cook the onion for 5–8 minutes until softened but not coloured. Add the remaining sauce ingredients and season well. Simmer for 10 minutes until the tomatoes are broken down and the sauce is thick. Check the seasoning.

Preheat the oven to 220°C/200°C fan/425°F/gas mark 7. Divide the dough into two pieces and roll each out into a circle about 26cm (10½in) wide. The dough is quite elastic, so take your time and let it rest between rolls if necessary. Gently press the dough into two 20cm (8in) loose-bottomed or springform cake tins. Fit it into the corners of the tins and press up the sides, making a crust about 3cm (1¼in) high. Trim off any excess.

Set aside 50g (1¾oz) of the mozzarella and lay the rest in a layer on the bottom of the pies. Sprinkle half of the Parmesan on to each pie, then spoon over the tomato sauce, spreading it to the edges. Sparingly, dot over the 'nduja and tear over the reserved mozzarella.

Bake for 30 minutes until the pizza base is crisp. Set aside to cool for 10 minutes, then remove from the pan, scatter with basil leaves and serve.

Serve with a fresh tomato and basil salad with a zingy dressing.

TOP TIP

THIS IS GREAT FOR USING UP THOSE SLIGHTLY 'OVER-SQUISHY' TOMATOES THAT YOU FIND LURKING AT THE BOTTOM OF YOUR FRIDGE SALAD DRAWER.

CHAR SIU PUFF

These are inspired by char siu sou, the roast pork pastry puffs found in many Chinese tea houses. Packed with delicious stickiness, they're perfect washed down with a nice little cup of Gunpowder tea.

2 x 320g (11½oz) packets of ready-rolled puff pastry

organic rapeseed oil, for greasing

1 free-range egg, beaten

FOR THE FILLING

600g (1lb 5oz) free-range pork collar

3 tablespoons local honey

1½ tablespoons brown sugar

2 teaspoons Chinese 5 spice

2 teaspoons chilli flakes

2 tablespoons hoisin sauce

2 tablespoons dark soy sauce

4 garlic cloves, grated to a paste

1 tablespoon sesame seeds

2 teaspoons sesame oil

2 spring onions, cut into 5cm (2in) lengths, then shredded lengthways

salt and freshly ground black pepper

FOR THE SHALLOTS

1 tablespoon organic rapeseed oil

4 echalion shallots, finely sliced

1 tablespoon brown sugar

2 teaspoons dark soy sauce

1 tablespoon oyster sauce

100ml (3½fl oz) chicken stock

Season the pork. Mix together half the honey with the sugar, Chinese 5 spice, chilli flakes, hoisin and soy sauces and garlic and marinate the pork, in the fridge, for 2 hours or overnight.

When ready to cook, preheat the oven to 160°C/140°C fan/325°F/gas mark 3. Remove the pork from the marinade, put it into a roasting dish and cook for 30 minutes.

Put the reserved marinade into a small saucepan, add the remaining honey and warm.

After 30 minutes, brush the pork all over with the marinade and roast for a further 20 minutes, then baste again and cook for another 20 minutes. Finally, baste with the last of the marinade and cook for 20 minutes.

While the pork is cooking, make the shallots. Heat the oil in a wok or large frying pan and stir-fry the shallots until they are softened. Add the sugar, soy and oyster sauces and chicken stock and cook for 2–4 minutes until it's reduced to a very sticky sauce. Set aside to cool.

Shred the pork in the pan it was cooked in so that it mixes with the sauce. Set aside to cool completely. Combine the shallots and pork and check the seasoning.

When ready, use an oven dish similar in size to the puff pastry sheets. Brush the dish with a little oil and line with a sheet of puff pastry. Spread the cooled pork mixture over the puff pastry. Lay the other sheet of pastry over the pork. Brush with beaten egg and sprinkle with sesame seeds, then refrigerate for 30 minutes.

Preheat the oven to 220°C/200°C fan/425°F/gas mark 7.

Using a sharp knife, slice parallel lines on the diagonal in one direction and then slice lines through them to make small diamonds (about 3 x 3cm/1¼ x 1¼in). Make sure that you slice all the way through both layers of pastry; this can take a few minutes to do neatly but it's worth the effort. Bake for 20–25 minutes, or until nicely browned.

Remove the tray from the oven and lightly brush with sesame oil. Leave the diamonds to cool slightly before removing them from the tin. Serve still warm, or cold later, scattered with the sliced spring onions.

TOP TIP! TO MAKE THE SPRING ONIONS CURL PRETTILY, SUBMERGE THEM IN ICED WATER, THEN DRY ON KITCHEN PAPER.

TOFU & SHIITAKE DIAMOND PUFF

Plant-based party food at its best; be sure to make enough for your carnivorous guests too – we guarantee they'll scoff them just as enthusiastically as the vegan contingent.

1 portion of vegan rough puff pastry (page 26)

melted plant-based butter, for brushing

plain flour, for dusting

FOR THE FILLING

8 tablespoons char siu sauce

4 teaspoons light soy sauce

6 teaspoons sesame oil

6cm (2½in) piece of fresh ginger, peeled and finely chopped

400g (14oz) block of tofu, drained, patted dry and cut into 5mm (¼in) dice

200g (7oz) shiitake mushrooms, cut into 5mm (¼in) dice

1 tablespoon sunflower oil

4 tablespoons panko breadcrumbs

3 spring onions, finely chopped

FOR THE SZECHUAN OIL

100ml (3½fl oz) neutral-tasting vegetable oil or peanut oil

2 teaspoons Szechuan pepper, lightly crushed in a pestle and mortar

1 star anise

½ teaspoon chilli flakes

2 teaspoons sesame seeds

1 teaspoon toasted sesame oil

¼ teaspoon maple syrup (optional)

For the filling, mix the char siu sauce, soy sauce, sesame oil and ginger in a shallow dish. Add the tofu and mushrooms and coat them in the marinade. Set aside for about 1 hour.

Preheat the oven to 200°C/180°C fan/400°F/gas mark 6. Brush a baking tray with sunflower oil and place in the oven.

Stir the breadcrumbs into the tofu and mushroom mixture. Once the baking tray is hot, tip the tofu and mushrooms into the tray in one layer and roast for 20–25 minutes, turning once, until nicely browned. Remove from the oven, stir through the chopped spring onions and leave to cool completely.

To make the Szechuan oil, heat the vegetable or peanut oil to 135°C (275°F) – use a cooking thermometer to check the temperature. Alternatively, if you don't have a thermometer, heat until you see wisps of smoke and then remove from the heat and leave to cool for 5 minutes.

Combine the Szechuan pepper, star anise and crushed chillies in a heatproof bowl that is large enough to contain the oil. When the oil reaches 135°C (275°F), pour it over the other ingredients. It will sizzle and become aromatic. The mixture will sizzle for a minute or so, then leave it to cool completely.

Dry-fry the sesame seeds in a small pan until lightly browned. Leave to cool, then stir into the Szechuan oil with the toasted sesame oil and maple syrup (if liked). Set aside.

Dust a work surface with flour and roll out the rough puff pastry to about 3mm (1¼in) thick. Slice the pastry to fit the base of your pie dish (we used a 29cm/11½in dish). Brush the pie dish with melted plant-based butter and place the sheet of puff pastry on top. Roll out another sheet of pastry to fit on top. Spread the cooled filling over the puff pastry, then top with the remaining pastry sheet. Brush with more melted plant-based butter, and then rest in the fridge for 30 minutes.

Preheat the oven to 220°C/200°C fan/425°F/gas mark 7.

Using a sharp knife, slice parallel lines on the diagonal in one direction and then slice lines through them to make small diamonds (about 3 x 3cm/¼ x 1¼in). Make sure that you slice all the way through both layers of pastry. Bake for about 20–25 minutes, or until nicely browned.

Remove the tray from the oven and lightly brush with the Szechuan oil to give a light sheen on top. Leave the diamonds to cool slightly before removing them from the tin. Serve still warm, or cold later.

TOP TIP

THE SZECHUAN OIL IS EVEN BETTER AFTER A FEW HOURS OR A DAY. STORE IT AT ROOM TEMPERATURE IN A NON-REACTIVE CONTAINER. ANY LEFTOVERS CAN BE USED AS A DRIZZLE ON OTHER RECIPES – IT'S BEST USED WITHIN A FEW WEEKS OF MAKING.

THE REUBEN

You guessed it; this one is inspired by our love of the iconic Reuben sandwich. There's been many a squabble about what makes the best Reuben but, for us, it has to be as heavy on the spices as the New York attitude. This isn't one to rustle up in minutes, it's about buying the best, sustainably produced beef you can and savouring every mouthful. We use regeneratively farmed Devonshire Longhorn.

½ **portion of mighty white pastry (page 24)**
plain flour, for dusting

FOR THE FILLING

1.5kg (3lb 5oz) beef short ribs (2 medium ribs)
1 litre (1¾ pints) beef stock
1 tablespoon black peppercorns
1 tablespoon coriander seeds
1 tablespoon fennel seeds
1 tablespoon smoked paprika
4 garlic cloves, peeled
1 tablespoon molasses
200g (7oz) sauerkraut, drained
200g (7oz) Emmental cheese, sliced
salt and freshly ground black pepper

FOR THE BÉCHAMEL

500ml (18fl oz) milk
1 bay leaf
5 black peppercorns
50g (1¾oz) butter
50g (1¾oz) plain flour
a few gratings of nutmeg
2 tablespoons English mustard

TO SERVE

sliced gherkins
sprigs of dill

Preheat the oven to 150°C/130°C fan/300°F/gas mark 2.

Using a large ovenproof casserole dish with a lid, pour the stock over the ribs and add the spices, garlic cloves and molasses. If you're lucky enough to have fresh stock, salt well. If using stock cubes, salt cautiously; you can always adjust later. Bring to a gentle simmer on the hob as you swirl and stir the liquid around the sides of the ribs, as best you can, to dissolve the molasses.

Put the lid on the pan and transfer to the oven for 3 hours or until the beef is very tender and falling off the bones. If the ribs aren't completely submerged in the stock, turn them halfway through the cooking.

Once cooked, remove from the oven to cool, then refrigerate with the lid on for a couple of hours or overnight, so the fat sets and you're able to lift it off and discard. (If you don't have time for that, skim the fat from the top of the cooking liquid with a spoon.)

Lift the ribs out on to a large plate and separate the meat from the bones and fat, then shred the meat into pieces. Sieve the liquid to remove the spices. Put the cooking liquid back into a pan on the hob and tip in the shredded meat. Bring to the boil and reduce until the liquid becomes a thick sauce coating the meat. Taste and season.

Take the pastry out of the fridge and unwrap. Dust your work surface and rolling pin with a little flour and roll the pastry out into a large rectangle slightly larger than a 32 x 22cm (12¾ x 8½in) shallow baking tin. We use a Swiss roll tin. Drape the pastry over the tin and gently push it into the corners. Chill for 30 minutes, then trim off any excess pastry.

Preheat the oven to 160°C/140°C fan/325°F/gas mark 3.

Line the pastry with baking parchment, fill with baking beans or rice and blind bake for 30 minutes until dry and lightly coloured. Remove from the oven, take out the parchment and beans and set aside.

While the pastry is cooking, make the béchamel. Heat the milk in a small pan with the bay leaf and peppercorns. Melt the butter in a saucepan and, when it's bubbling, stir in the flour and cook, stirring, for a minute. Slowly add the warm milk (discard the bay leaf and peppercorns), stirring after each addition until the mixture is smooth. Add the nutmeg and mustard, season and stir well. Cover the surface of the sauce with wax wrap and set aside to cool a little.

When the pastry is cooled, spread the béchamel over the pie case, then layer over the shredded beef, sauerkraut, and top with the sliced cheese. Return to the oven for 25 minutes until the cheese has melted and the pie is hot through. Scatter, flamboyantly, with sliced gherkins and sprigs of dill and serve with your best 'New Yoik' accent.

THE REUBENO

No compromises: this plant-based Reubeno packs as much of a punch as its meaty brother (see opposite). Stuffed to the New York loft rafters with big flavours and spices, and a huge helping of chutzpah!

½ **portion of mighty white pastry (page 24)**

plain flour, for dusting

FOR THE FILLING

500ml (18fl oz) hot vegetable stock

1 tablespoon black peppercorns

1 tablespoon coriander seeds

1 tablespoon fennel seeds

1 tablespoon smoked paprika

4 garlic cloves, bashed

1 tablespoon brown sugar

25g (1oz) dried porcini mushrooms

2 tablespoons olive oil

1 large onion, finely sliced

1 tablespoon balsamic vinegar

400g (14oz) king oyster mushrooms, washed and dried

150g (5½oz) sauerkraut, drained

100g (3½oz) plant-based cheese, grated

salt and freshly ground black pepper

FOR THE BÉCHAMEL

300g (10½oz) silken tofu, well drained

30g (1oz) white miso paste

40g (1½oz) nutritional yeast

2 tablespoons olive oil

2 teaspoons onion granules

2 teaspoons garlic granules

¼ nutmeg, finely grated

2 tablespoons English mustard

To SERVE

sprigs of dill

gherkins

Combine the hot stock with all of the spices, garlic and sugar, stir to dissolve the sugar, then add the dried mushrooms and set aside to soak for 30 minutes.

Gently heat the oil in a large, heavy-based pan. Add the onion to the pan with the balsamic vinegar, season and cook gently for 15 minutes until deep brown and well caramelized.

Use a fork to score the stems of the oyster mushrooms, then pull apart into shreds. Throw them into the saucepan with the onions. Add a little more oil if necessary and cook the mushrooms with the onions for 3–5 minutes until they're softened.

Once the porcini have soaked, strain the liquor into a jug, pick out the mushrooms, chop and add them to the pan with the fresh mushrooms. Discard the spices and pour the liquor in with the mushrooms. Heat to a simmer, then allow to reduce until you have a thick sticky mixture. Taste and season.

Preheat the oven to 160°C/140°C fan/325°F/gas mark 3.

Dust a work surface with flour and roll out the pastry into a large rectangle slightly larger than a 32 x 22cm (12¾ x 8½in) shallow baking tin, like a brownie tin or small roasting pan. Carefully lift the pastry and drape it over the tin, gently pressing into the corners. Trim off any excess. The pastry can be a little crumbly but, don't worry, if there's any tears just patch it up, no one will know! Line the pastry with baking parchment, fill with baking beans or rice and blind bake for 30 minutes until dry and lightly coloured. Remove from the oven, take out the parchment and beans and set aside.

To make the béchamel, put all the ingredients in a blender, season with salt and pepper and blend until smooth. Spread the béchamel sauce over the pastry base, top with the sticky mushroom mix and sauerkraut, and then sprinkle over the cheese. Return to the oven for 25 minutes until the cheese has melted (though it won't melt like dairy cheese). When ready to serve, top with plenty of dill and gherkins.

THERE ARE MANY GREAT INDEPENDENT VEGAN CHEESEMAKERS THESE DAYS, BUT IF YOU CAN'T FIND ONE YOU CAN USE SUPERMARKET PLANT-BASED CHEESE OR JUST LEAVE IT OUT. IT'LL STILL TASTE GREAT!

MIND YOUR TEMPEH!

BEAN-BASED BRILLIANCE

A few years ago, we experimented with tempeh, trialling it in a new pie recipe. The results were disastrous. But we couldn't fill a book with sustainable recipes without giving it another chance. After all, it's about as good a high-protein, low-carbon ingredient as you can get.

But after our last calamitous encounter with it, we needed to enlist the help of some tempehxperts (sorry). So as big fans of a pun-based brand name, we got in touch with Benedict Meade, owner of Tempeh Meades (based just behind Bristol's Temple Meads train station!).

Ben has turned us into tempeh converts; it turns out that not all tempeh is made equal. Unlike the mass-produced stuff we'd used before, Ben takes it slow, fermenting the beans at a lower temperature over two days instead of one, and in two stages: first a lactoferment, then the main cultured fermentation.

It's worth mentioning that he always uses organic soya beans from Europe, which is a big plus-point, as irresponsible soya production in Asia

and Central America can often be fraught with deforestation issues. Something we talk about a little more on page 30.

Because Ben's tempeh is made in super-small batches, he's able to babysit his beans while the fermentation's happening to ensure they are at just the right temperature for just the right amount of time.

We also learned that tempeh should either be enjoyed within a few days of fermenting – or is best stored frozen. This eliminates the two main problems with long-life pasteurized tempeh: the bitter flavour which emerges during storage, and an overly dense, unappetising texture.

It's the amazingly good texture of Ben's unpasteurized tempeh that works so well in our Pide Piper recipe on page 78, providing the perfect plant-based alternative to lamb or beef mince, while soaking up the recipe's heady mix of herbs and spices.

THE PIDE PIPER

Inspired by pide, the boat-shaped pockets of deliciousness which are often described as Turkish pizza. Here we've switched out the bread dough for rough puff, and the often used beef or lamb mince for chopped tempeh, which works really well. The trick with a pide filling is to go hard (or go home) with the spices, you almost need to 'over season' the 'mince', as it is just a base which you then slather with yogurt, herbs and other sprinkly bits for freshness.

½ **portion of vegan rough puff pastry (page 26)**

plain flour, for dusting

FOR THE FILLING

3 red onions, finely sliced

100ml (3½fl oz) red wine vinegar

1 teaspoon sugar

½ teaspoon salt

2 teaspoons pink peppercorns

2 tablespoons organic rapeseed oil

2 teaspoons paprika

2 teaspoons allspice

1 teaspoon ground cumin

2 teaspoons sumac

2 hot green chillies, deseeded and finely diced

2 garlic cloves, crushed

250g (9oz) tempeh, grated or crumbled

400ml (14fl oz) vegetable stock

2 teaspoons date molasses

1 bay leaf

4 tablespoons unsweetened plant-based yogurt, plus a little extra to serve

1 tablespoon dark tahini

salt and freshly ground black pepper

To SERVE

chopped flat-leaf parsley

sesame seeds

lemon wedges

pickled chillies

Combine one of the red onions with the vinegar, sugar, salt and pink peppercorns. Stir well and set aside.

Heat 1 tablespoon of the oil in a heavy-based saucepan and gently cook the remaining onions for 8–10 minutes until soft. Stir in the spices, then add the chilli and garlic and continue to cook for a further 2–3 minutes. Stir in the tempeh so it becomes coated with spices, then add the vegetable stock, molasses and bay leaf. Season well and cook for 5–6 minutes until the liquid is absorbed. Remove the bay leaf and set aside.

Preheat the oven to 180°C/160°C fan/350°F/gas mark 4. Line a baking tray with baking parchment.

Dust a work surface with flour and roll out the pastry to 3mm (1/8in) thick. Cut in half, then cut each half into a long boat shape, pointed at the ends and wide in the middle. Lay on the lined baking tray.

Combine the yogurt and tahini and season. Spread this mixture over the pastry, leaving a 2cm (¾in) border around the edges. Pile the tempeh mixture on top of the yogurt, then fold and crimp the edges of the pastry so that they come up slightly overlapping the tempeh. Brush with the remaining oil.

Bake in the oven for 20 minutes. When ready to serve, top with the pink onions, scatter with parsley and sesame seeds and drizzle with any leftover yogurt. Serve with lemon wedges and pickled chillies on the side.

TOP TIP

SEE PAGE 26 FOR IDEAS ON HOW TO USE UP ANY OFFCUT PASTRY – OR FEEL FREE TO FREESTYLE WITH THE SHAPE OF THE 'BOAT' TO MINIMIZE THE LEFTOVERS (RECTANGLES WORK TOO – IT DOESN'T HAVE TO FLOAT!)

ANA'S LAMB SAUSAGE BÖREK

Tris's first music tour (as a chef) was with the Pet Shop Boys. All was going swimmingly until they reached the Czech Republic, and the Head Chef went AWOL! There were 70 hungry mouths to feed, and very little time. A runaway nun from Serbia called Ana stepped in and offered to knock up a few böreks using what they had in their flight cases, and this is based on that life-saving recipe.

7 x A4-sized sheets of foodie pastry (page 22)

FOR THE FILLING

2 tablespoons olive oil, plus extra for brushing and greasing

2 red onions, diced

50g (1¾oz) pine nuts

½ pointed or Savoy cabbage, core removed, halved and very finely sliced (about 400g/14oz total weight)

1 tablespoon white or red wine vinegar 4 garlic cloves, crushed

6 merguez sausages

zest of 1 lemon

25g (1oz) parsley, large stalks removed and coarsely chopped

3 sprigs of mint, leaved picked and finely sliced

50g (1¾oz) panko breadcrumbs

FOR THE GLAZE

2 sprigs of mint

1 preserved lemon, coarsely chopped

2 tablespoons sugar

4 tablespoons boiling water

2 teaspoons cumin seeds

2 teaspoons fennel seeds

To make the filling, heat the oil in a frying pan and gently cook the onions and pine nuts for 10 minutes. Add the cabbage, vinegar and a splash of water and put a lid on. Cook for 8–10 minutes, stirring occasionally. Stir in the garlic, then increase the heat and cook for 3–4 minutes until it starts to brown. Transfer to a large bowl and set aside to cool.

Remove the sausage meat from the skins and, when the cabbage mixture has cooled a little, use your hands to mix it into the cabbage, along with the lemon zest, herbs, breadcrumbs and vinegar. Allow to cool completely.

Preheat the oven to 180°C/160°C fan/350°F/gas mark 4.

Clear a long space on your work surface and lay out four sheets of pastry, with the longest side closest to you. Brush each sheet lightly with olive oil and overlap each sheet by 5cm (2in). Take another sheet and place it, shortest side towards you, centrally on the top of the four sheets, covering the middle seam, and brush this with oil. Place the remaining two sheets, the same way over the other seams on either side, overlapping the central sheet by 5cm (2in) on both sides, and lightly oil both of these. The aim is to make a long strip of pastry (see the sketch on the bottom left of the page).

Take your cooled mixture and form into a 2cm (¾in) thick sausage. Place this on the pastry, 5cm (2in) from the base of the sheet – it should fill the length of the pastry. There will be a sheet of pastry sticking out at either side – trim off this excess and reserve for patching any cracks in the filo. Fold the bottom of the pastry up and over the mixture, tucking it tightly to form a sausage. Keep rolling until you reach the top – the mixture should be fully encased, and you should have a long filo sausage. Start at one end and gently curl inwards to form a spiral; keep going until a large spiral is formed. If the pastry breaks or cracks, cover the cracks with any reserved pastry. Place the pastry spiral into an oiled 23cm (9in) springform cake tin, brush lightly with olive oil and bake in the oven for 1 hour until golden and crisp.

If you don't have a cake tin, this can be baked on a flat baking sheet or in an ovenproof frying pan. Start checking it after 45 minutes of cooking to ensure the pastry doesn't burn on the sides.

While the börek is cooking, combine all the glaze ingredients, except the seeds. After 1 hour, remove the börek from the oven, brush with the glaze and sprinkle with the seeds. Return to the oven for 10 minutes.

Remove from the oven and allow to cool in the tin for 10 minutes before turning on to a plate. Delicious served warm or at room temperature if not served immediately. Serve with garlicky greens.

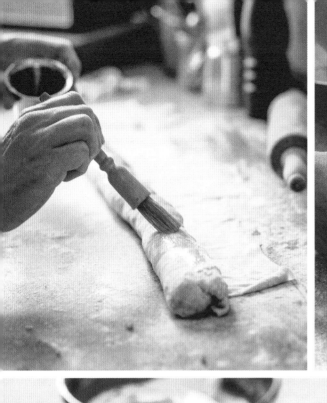

SPINACH & CHARD SPIRAL

This vegan börek is inspired by that magical part of the world where the Mediterranean meets Asia. Za'atar, lemon zest, plant-based feta and mint take the leafy green filling to new levels of fresh summery tangy-ness. A real party piece, your guests (vegans and carnivores alike) will devour it, but not before they've been wowed by its beauty.

7 x A4-sized sheets of foodle pastry (page 22)

FOR THE FILLING

300g (10½oz) spinach

400g (14oz) rainbow or Swiss chard, leaves separated, and stalks finely sliced

100g (3½oz) jarred artichoke hearts in oil, roughly chopped

4 tablespoons olive oil, plus extra for brushing and greasing

1 large shallot or ½ white onion, finely diced

6 garlic cloves, crushed

6 spring onions, finely sliced

50g (1¾oz) pine nuts, lightly toasted in a dry pan

100g (3½oz) plant-based cream cheese

1 tablespoon za'atar, plus extra for sprinkling

zest of 1 lemon

3 sprigs of mint, leaves picked and finely chopped

300g (10½oz) plant-based feta, crumbled

¼ nutmeg, grated, or a pinch of ground nutmeg

salt and freshly ground black pepper

Place a large frying pan over a medium heat and wilt the spinach and chard leaves in batches. Once wilted, remove to a colander to cool. Once cool, use your hands to squeeze the excess water from the leaves, then place in a clean tea towel and squeeze again to remove as much excess water as possible. Coarsely chop the leaves and set aside.

Return the pan to the heat, pour in 2 tablespoons of oil from the jar of artichokes and 2 tablespoons of olive oil, then add the shallot and finely sliced chard stalks and cook for 10 minutes until translucent. Add the garlic, spring onions and pine nuts, season with salt and pepper and cook for a further 10 minutes. Add the spinach, chard leaves and artichoke hearts, mix thoroughly, cook until warmed through, then add the cream cheese, allowing it to melt through the mixture. Remove the pan from the heat and add the za'atar, lemon zest, mint and crumbled feta, mix and allow to cool completely.

Preheat the oven to 180°C/160°C fan/350°F/gas mark 4.

Clear a long space on your work surface and lay out four sheets of pastry, with the longest side closest to you. Brush each sheet lightly with olive oil and overlap each sheet by 5cm (2in). Take another sheet and place it, shortest side towards you, centrally on the top of the four sheets, covering the middle seam, and brush this with oil. Place the remaining two sheets, the same way over the other seams on either side, overlapping the central sheet by 5cm (2in) on both sides, and lightly oil both of these. The aim is to make a long strip of pastry (see the sketch on the bottom left of the page).

Take your cooled filling mixture and form into a 2cm (¾in) thick sausage. Place this on the pastry, 5cm (2in) from the base of the filo sheet – it should fill the length of the pastry. Trim off 5cm (2in) from each side of the base filo pastry sheet (reserve for patching any cracks in the filo) and then fold the remaining base layer over each end of the mixture. Fold the bottom 5cm (2in) flap up and over the mixture, tucking it tightly to form a sausage. Keep rolling until you reach the top – the mixture should be fully encased, and you should have a long filo sausage. Start at one end and gently curl inwards to form a spiral; keep going until a large spiral is formed. If the pastry breaks or cracks, wrap sections of the reserved oiled pieces of pastry around them.

Place the pastry spiral into an oiled 23cm (9in) springform cake tin, brush lightly with olive oil and sprinkle with some za'atar. Bake in the oven for 1 hour until golden and crisp. Remove from the oven and allow to cool in the tin for 10 minutes before removing to a plate. Delicious served warm or at room temperature if not serving immediately.

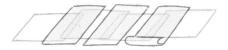

DATE & OAT FLAPJACK

When is a pie not a pie? When it's a flapjack! We somehow sneaked this past our editor because who doesn't love something that's oaty, caramelly, fruity and fudgy? You can use any dried fruit you have..

300g (10½oz) soft dried fruit,
    such as Medjool dates, apricots
    or apples

300ml (10fl oz) boiling water

1 teaspoon bicarbonate of soda

200g (7oz) golden syrup

250g (9oz) plant-based butter

250g (9oz) soft light brown sugar

400g (14oz) rolled oats

80g (2¾oz) seeds of your choice,
    such as sunflower, pumpkin
    or linseed

Chop the dried fruit and put in a bowl with the boiling water, the bicarb and half the golden syrup. Stir until the syrup has dissolved and leave to soak for 10 minutes.

Transfer the fruit mixture to a saucepan and simmer for about 10 minutes until it becomes thick and jammy. Set aside.

Preheat the oven to 180°C/160°C fan/350°F/gas mark 4 and line a 20cm (8in) square baking tray with greaseproof paper.

In another saucepan, melt together the remaining syrup, the plant-based butter and sugar. Put the oats in a bowl and pour over the butter mixture. Stir well until it is incorporated.

Tip half of the oats into the baking tray and press into the corners, then pour over the fruit mixture and spread out evenly over the oat layer. Add the seeds to the remaining oats and stir well. Carefully and evenly, cover the fruit layer with the remaining oats and bake for 30 minutes.

Leave to cool in the tin, then turn out and cut into 12 squares. These will keep in an airtight container for up to a week but will most likely be devoured long before then!

ECO POINTS

THINK TWICE ABOUT BUYING SOMETHING SHROUDED IN SINGLE-USE PLASTIC. INSTEAD, REPURPOSE OLD POTS, TUBS, TINS AND JARS FOR STORAGE. OLD IS THE NEW 'NEW'.

AUTUMN FRUIT COBBLER

This particular cobbler is a celebration of autumn, a final fruity fling before winter sets in. But you can use any fruit depending on the season – they all taste amazing with a mouthful of steaming scone topping. We like to think the name 'cobbler' comes from the fact that the crust looks like cobble stones (and that by using the word 'crust' here we can claim this is a pie...).

FOR THE SCONE TOP

200g (7oz) self-raising flour, plus extra for dusting

½ teaspoon bicarbonate of soda

80g (2¾oz) plant-based margarine

2 tablespoons caster sugar

80ml (2½fl oz) oat milk, plus extra for brushing

2 tablespoons demerara sugar

FOR THE FRUITY BOTTOM

600g (1lb 5oz) apples, peeled and chopped

400g (14oz) blackberries

OR 1kg (2lb 4oz) of any fruit in season or going off in the fruit bowl

100g (3½oz) granulated or caster sugar

10g (¼oz) cornflour

1 vanilla pod

2 bay leaves

Start by making the scones. Put the flour and bicarb in a large bowl, then rub in the margarine with your fingertips until there are no lumps. Stir in the caster sugar, then make a well in the centre of the flour mix and add the oat milk. Using a table knife, make a cutting motion through the mixture to start to combine the milk and dry ingredients. As it starts to come together, use your hands to bring it into a ball of dough. Cover in wax wrap and refrigerate for 30 minutes.

Preheat the oven to 200°C/180°C fan/400°F/gas mark 6.

Meanwhile, put the fruit in a baking dish and sprinkle over the sugar and cornflour. Split the vanilla pod and scrape out the seeds and dot them over the fruit, then tuck the pod and bay leaves in amongst the fruit too.

Put in the oven for 20 minutes to start the cooking process. When the scone mix has chilled, unwrap it and, on a floured surface, pat out to about 2cm (¾in) thick. Use a 5cm (2in) pastry cutter to cut circular scones, then gather the leftover dough together and repeat until all the dough is used.

Take the fruit out of the oven, discard the vanilla pod and bay leaves, and gently place the scones on top. Brush with a little extra oat milk and sprinkle with the demerara. Return to the oven for a further 25–30 minutes until the fruit is bubbling and the scones are puffed up and browned.

DELICIOUS WITH OUR PLANT-BASED CUSTARD ON PAGE 181.

PIE NA COLADA

A tropical island fantasy full of fruit and sunshine, this is a kitsch'd up tarte Tatin. Coconut, rum and pineapple definitely deliver on the palm-fringed beach vibes, but we recommend dialling things up with cocktail umbrellas, glacé cherries and a can of squirty cream.

320g (11½oz) packet of ready-rolled puff pastry

FOR THE FILLING

1 medium ripe pineapple

4 tablespoons brown sugar

60g (2¼oz) unsalted butter, softened

75ml (2½fl oz) spiced rum

2 teaspoons mixed spice

a small bunch of fresh mint, finely sliced

a small bunch of basil leaves, finely sliced

zest of 2 limes

2 tablespoons desiccated coconut, toasted

vanilla ice cream, to serve

Cut the top and bottom off the pineapple and peel off the skin with a serrated knife. Slice into 1cm (½in) slices, cut each slice in half to make a semicircle, then, with a pastry cutter, remove the core of each slice.

Put the brown sugar, butter, rum, the mixed spice and half the herbs into a heavy-based saucepan and melt together. Bring to the boil for 1–3 minutes or until syrupy, then add the pineapple slices to the pan and cook over a low heat for 5 minutes, turning the pineapple over several times to coat it in the caramel.

Preheat the oven to 180°C/160°C fan/350°F/gas mark 4.

Unroll the puff pastry and cut around a 25cm (9in) ovenproof frying pan to make a large circle of pastry. Spread half the caramel around the bottom of the pan, then arrange the pineapple slices, slightly overlapping so that they all fit in well. Lay the pastry over the top and tuck in the edges, then bake for 20–25 minutes until the pastry is puffed up and golden.

While the tart is cooking, make the topping by combining the lime zest, desiccated coconut and remaining herbs.

Once the Tatin is cooked, allow to stand for 10 minutes, then invert it on to a serving plate.

Reheat the remaining caramel and pour over, then top with the coconut mixture. Serve with scoops of vanilla ice cream.

CIAO!

SERVE WITH A CUBA LIBRE, WHICH WE REALIZE IS NOT FROM THE SAME ISLAND AS THE PIÑA COLADA (CUBA AND PUERTO RICO, RESPECTIVELY) BUT IT USES UP THOSE LEFTOVER LIMES!

TOO GOOD TO WASTE

IT'S RIDICULOUS; 8-10% OF GLOBAL GREENHOUSE GAS EMISSIONS ARE ASSOCIATED WITH FOOD THAT NEVER GETS EATEN.

Put another way, one third of food produced is never eaten, and to produce this much wasted food would use a land mass the size of China. Population growth and food security concerns are just two of the many undisputable reasons why we can't afford to let this madness continue.

Food waste is a great example of an environmental problem that can feel unsurmountable and overwhelming. In these cases, we reckon the best thing to do is focus on changing the things that are in our control.

And when you think that in the UK, one household wastes on average the equivalent of eight meals a week, this is definitely on us. (FYI that's an area almost the size of Wales – around 19,000km – needed to produce the food and drink wasted!)

So, all the recipes in this book are designed to keep food waste to a minimum. You'll find no carrots peeled or outer leaves discarded here!

This sort of cooking is slowly becoming more mainstream, which will surely help us bring the number of wasted meals per household down.

But what else can we do?

BOO!

DO THE PIE THING

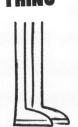

HERE ARE JUST A FEW IDEAS TO GET YOU STARTED:

- Up your freezer game. Instead of letting things slowly go off in the fridge, box it up and put it in the freezer to get a few more months on the clock. Great for excess fresh chopped herbs and meal leftovers.

- Pickle leftover vegetables like cucumber, cabbage, cauliflower for use in salads and sandwiches over the next few months. Likewise turn mushy fruit and berries into jam or compote to shove on yogurt or porridge.

- Treat Best Before dates as a guide rather than a rule. Trust your primal super-power to see or smell when something's past its best.

- Buy with intent to ensure you're not buying to throw away. It's true what people say about food shopping on an empty stomach – make sure it's your head making the decisions…!

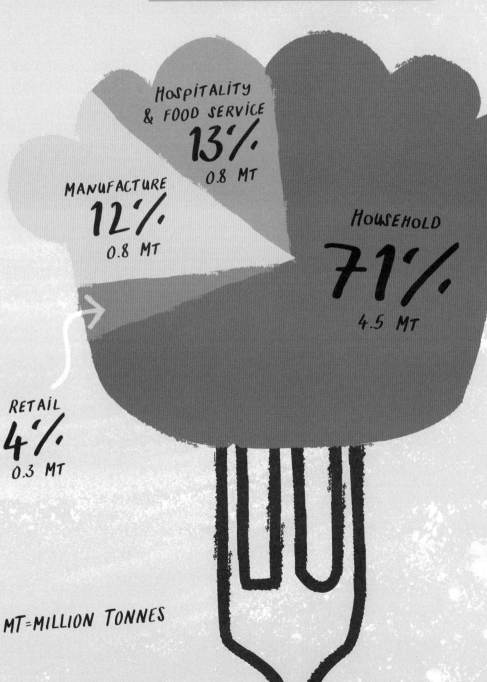

AMOUNT of WASTED FOOD in THE UK
(AFTER iT'S LEFT THE FARM)

HospiTALiTY
& FOOD SERViCE
13%
0.8 MT

MANUFACTURE
12%
0.8 MT

HOUSEHOLD
71%
4.5 MT

RETAiL
4%
0.3 MT

MT=MILLION TONNES

IT'S CRAZY THAT SO MANY FRESH
FOODS CARRY UNNECESSARY OR OVER-
CAUTIOUS DATE LABELLING. EXTENDING
PRODUCT LIFE BY ONLY 24 HOURS
COULD PREVENT 250,000 TONNES
OF FOOD FROM BEING WASTED!

OTHER TOP & POT PIES

PASTA-TOPPED, POTATO-TOPPED & SAUCY-TOPPED DELIGHTS

SO NACHO PIE

When Tris was Head Chef at Jon's London pub in the 90s, pile upon pile of 'Nachos Grande' were sold every day. They were THE favourite sharing dish (and quite exotic back then!). Now we've resurrected them in pie form here. Don't attempt to eat it with cutlery...

400g (14oz) butternut squash, peeled and cut into 3cm (1¼in) cubes

4 tablespoons organic rapeseed oil

1 dried ancho chilli

1 dried guajillo or pasilla chilli

300ml (10fl oz) boiling vegetable stock

1 large brown onion, finely sliced

2 garlic cloves, crushed

1 cinnamon stick

1 bay leaf

1 teaspoon smoked paprika

1 teaspoon ground cumin

1 teaspoon dried oregano

2 tablespoons tomato purée

1 tablespoon red wine vinegar

1 teaspoon sugar

400g (14oz) can chopped tomatoes

400g (14oz) can pinto or borlotti beans, drained and rinsed

1–3 large flour tortilla wraps

salt and freshly ground black pepper

FOR THE TOPPING

1 flour tortilla, cut into triangles

¼ teaspoon ground cumin

¼ teaspoon smoked paprika

¼ teaspoon garlic granules

1 tablespoon organic rapeseed oil

150g (5½oz) Cheddar or plant-based cheese, grated

TO SERVE

4 medium tomatoes, finely diced

1 small white onion, finely diced

1 jalapeño or serrano chilli, very finely diced

20g (¾oz) coriander leaves, finely chopped

juice of 1 lime

3 tablespoons sour cream or plant-based alternative

Preheat the oven to 200°C/180°C fan/400°F/gas mark 6.

Toss the butternut squash in 2 tablespoons of the oil and season with salt and pepper, spread on a baking tray and roast in the oven for 30 minutes. When tender and caramelizing on the edges, remove from the oven and set aside. Reduce the oven temperature to 180°C/160°C fan/350°F/gas mark 4.

Tear the dried chillies into strips, remove and discard the stalks and seeds. Place in a jug and pour over the vegetable stock. Leave to soak for 20 minutes and then use a stick blender to blend to a smooth paste and set aside.

Heat the remaining 2 tablespoons of oil in a heavy-based casserole dish over a medium heat and, when hot, add the onion and cook for 15–20 minutes until golden and caramelized. Add the garlic, cinnamon stick and bay leaf, season with salt and pepper, and cook for 2 minutes until fragrant. Add the paprika, cumin, oregano and tomato purée and cook for a further 2 minutes, then add the red wine vinegar and allow to bubble down and reduce. Add the chilli paste, sugar and the can of tomatoes. Bring to a simmer and cook for 5 minutes before adding the drained beans and roasted butternut squash, then cook over a low heat for a further 30 minutes until the sauce is reduced and thick. Take off the heat to cool slightly and remove and discard the cinnamon stick and bay leaf.

Take a round pie dish that fits your tortilla wrap or a metal-handled ovenproof frying pan.

In a bowl, combine the tortilla triangles with the spices and oil and toss together, then mix in a third of the grated cheese. Press a whole flour tortilla into the base of the pan, if your pan is large, use the extra 2 tortillas and overlap them to ensure the edges overhang. Place half your warm butternut and bean filling into the case (you won't need all of it) and sprinkle over a third of the grated cheese, top with the spiced tortilla triangles and finish with the remaining grated cheese. Bake in the oven for 20 minutes until the cheese is bubbling and golden.

To serve, combine the diced tomato, onion, chilli, coriander and lime juice with a pinch of salt to make a salsa. Spoon this on top of the pie along with the sour cream and serve.

The remaining filling can be served with rice if you don't fancy making another pie, or frozen for up to 6 months.

CHILLI CON CARNAGE

**Not for the faint-hearted, this filthy beast of a pie is gonna make you sweat.
Beneath the oozy, bubbly mac 'n' cheese lurks a fruity Scotch bonnet chilli
so hot it'll blow more than your socks off... You've been warned.
Let the carnage commence!**

1 tablespoon organic rapeseed oil

750g (1lb 10oz) beef mince

400g (14oz) smoked lardons

1 onion, finely diced

2 garlic cloves, crushed

2 carrots, washed and finely diced

1 green pepper, deseeded
and diced

1 Scotch bonnet chilli, seeds
discarded, finely diced

1 teaspoon chilli powder
(as hot as you dare)

2 teaspoons smoked paprika

2 teaspoons ground cumin

2 teaspoons chipotle paste

2 tablespoons tomato purée

2 tablespoons plain flour

150ml (5fl oz) dark ale

400g (14oz) can chopped tomatoes

400g (14oz) can red kidney beans,
drained

1 tablespoon dried oregano

500ml (18fl oz) beef or
vegetable stock

50g (1¾oz) fresh or dried
breadcrumbs

50g (1¾oz) Somerset
Cheddar, grated

salt and freshly ground
black pepper

FOR THE MAC 'N' CHEESE

200g (7oz) macaroni

50g (1¾oz) unsalted butter

50g (1¾oz) plain flour

500ml (18fl oz) milk

a few gratings of nutmeg

1 teaspoon English mustard

100g (3½oz) Cheddar, grated

Heat the oil in a large saucepan, add the mince and brown well over a high heat until nicely caramelized. Remove the meat to a plate, with a slotted spoon. Repeat with the lardons until crisp. Put half of the lardons with the mince and set aside the rest for the topping.

Reduce the heat to medium–low and add the onion, garlic, carrots and green pepper to the pan, stir well, put on the lid and cook for 8–10 minutes, stirring occasionally. Sprinkle in as much of the Scotch bonnet as you dare, the chilli powder, paprika and cumin and stir in the chipotle paste. Cook for a minute. Return the beef and lardons to the pan. Stir in the tomato purée, then sprinkle over the flour, stir and cook for 1–2 minutes.

Pour in the ale and stir well. Add the chopped tomatoes, kidney beans along with the oregano and continue to stir as you add the stock. Season well and leave to cook for 1 hour, uncovered.

To make the mac 'n' cheese, cook the macaroni according to the packet instructions.

For the cheese sauce, melt the butter in a saucepan and, when it's foaming, add the flour and cook over a medium heat, stirring continuously, for 3–4 minutes. Slowly add the milk, stirring with each addition. It may look lumpy at first but keep beating with a wooden spoon or whisk and it will become smooth. Once all the milk is added, keep stirring as it comes to a simmer. Add the nutmeg, mustard and cheese and season. Stir until everything is incorporated and the sauce is thick.

Preheat the oven to 220°C/200°C fan/425°F/gas mark 6. Drain the macaroni well, return it to the pan, then pour over two-thirds of the cheese sauce and mix well to coat. Transfer the chilli to a large ovenproof dish and carefully top with the mac 'n' cheese. Pour over the remaining cheese sauce.

Combine the remaining lardons with the breadcrumbs and Cheddar. Sprinkle this over the macaroni and bake in the oven for 20–25 minutes until the top is crispy and browned and the sauce is bubbling. Serve with fennel slaw and some habanero sour cream.

JACKFRUIT IS A GREAT REPLACEMENT FOR THE BEEF IN THIS RECIPE IF YOU FANCY A CHANGE. USE 2 PORTIONS OF THE JACKFRUIT RECIPE ON PAGE 180.

JACK YOUR BODY

MIGHTY APHRODITE

A great way to showcase our perfect plant-based béchamel recipe, it sits atop a rich Grecian-inspired Puy lentil stew here. You'll never bother with a meat Moussaka again.

6 tablespoons olive oil

4 aubergines, cut into 5mm (¼in) slices from root to tip

1 onion, finely diced

2 garlic cloves, crushed

2 sprigs of rosemary, picked and finely chopped

1 teaspoon ground cinnamon

½ teaspoon chilli flakes

2 tablespoons tomato purée

250ml (9fl oz) red wine

400g (14oz) can cherry tomatoes, drained of liquid

250g (9oz) ready-cooked Puy lentils

2 sun-dried tomatoes, finely chopped

200g (7oz) roasted red peppers, roughly chopped

50g (1¾oz) Kalamata olives, pitted and roughly chopped

200g (7oz) block of plant-based feta, crumbled

1 tablespoon pumpkin seeds

salt and freshly ground black pepper

FOR THE BÉCHAMEL

300g (10½oz) silken tofu, well drained

30g (1oz) white miso paste

40g (1½oz) nutritional yeast

2 tablespoons olive oil

2 teaspoons onion granules

2 teaspoons garlic granules

¼ nutmeg, finely grated

FOR THE TZATZIKI

1 medium cucumber, peeled, seeds removed and coarsely grated

250g (9oz) plant-based yogurt

25g (1oz) mint leaves, finely shredded

1 garlic clove, crushed

½ teaspoon salt

juice of ½ lemon

Preheat the oven to 200°C/180°C fan/400°F/gas mark 6.

Use 4 tablespoons of the oil to oil both sides of each aubergine slice using a pastry brush. Arrange on two baking sheets, ensuring that the slices don't overlap, and season well with salt and pepper. Roast in the oven for 40 minutes–1 hour until golden, turning the slices halfway through cooking. Remove from the oven and set aside; this mixture should be warm for the pie assembly.

Heat the remaining 2 tablespoons of oil in a heavy-based casserole dish over a medium heat and, when hot, add the onion and cook for 5 minutes until translucent, then add the garlic, rosemary, cinnamon and chilli flakes, season with salt and pepper and cook for 2 minutes. Add the tomato purée, stirring to combine, and cook for a further 2 minutes, then increase the heat, pour in the red wine and simmer to reduce. Once reduced by half, add the drained tomatoes and simmer for a further 5 minutes. Add the lentils, sun-dried tomatoes, red peppers and olives. Simmer for 20 minutes until the sauce is reduced and thickened. Remove from the heat and set aside.

To make the béchamel, place all the ingredients in a blender, season with salt and pepper and blend until smooth.

To assemble the pie, spoon one third of the mixture into your pie dish, top with a third of the crumbled feta and arrange a layer of roasted aubergine slices on top. Repeat this arrangement twice more, finishing with a layer of aubergine. Pour your béchamel on top, adding a couple of extra rasps of nutmeg and some cracked black pepper. Sprinkle over the pumpkin seeds and cook in the oven for 40 minutes until bubbling and golden on top.

To make the tzatziki, squeeze the grated cucumber to remove as much excess water as possible and then mix together with the remaining ingredients. Allow to sit for 10 minutes and then serve alongside the pie.

PEAS & LOVE   SAVE THE DRAINED TOMATO JUICE FOR USE IN A SOUP OR QUICK PASTA SAUCE.

THE VICTORY BAP

WHEN BURGERS & PIES COLLIDE

In 2022, Bristol's Beef Chucky 2.0 from Danny's Burgers took the Best Burger title in the National Burger Awards just weeks after the British Pie Awards crowned our GF Mooless Moo the Supreme Champion, 'Pie of Pies'. A celebration-collaboration felt like the most fitting way to mark the city's double triumph, so for one night only, Danny's and Pieminister joined forces to craft one mighty creation – the Victory Bap.

Built from the bottom up, this Burger-Piebrid involved stacking two native-breed, 50-day dry-aged beef patties, braised and smoked chuck steak, American cheese, our signature gravy, beer cheese sauce, pickled red onions and candied jalapeños inside a crispy onion pie crust. Topped off with a brioche bun lid and speared together with a free-range British corn dog skewer.

Let this page be the nudge you need to create your own pie x something else hybrid at home.

FREE RANGE
CORN DOG

BRIOCHE BUN

CANDIED
JALAPEÑOS

PICKLED
RED ONIONS

BEER CHEESE
SAUCE

PIEMINISTER
GRAVY

AGED BRITISH
BEEF PATTY

AMERICAN
CHEESE

BRAISED SMOKED
CHUCK STEAK

AGED BRITISH
BEEF PATTY

BURNT BUTTER
& ONION
PASTRY PIE CASE

MATADOR

A unique take on our beloved Matador Pie which has been part of the Pieminister range since we began, here it's finished with a crunchy patatas bravas-style top. Once you've made the stew (the time-consuming bit) this dish can be quickly assembled the next day. In fact – you've guessed it – the flavours of the stew meld even better when it's left for a bit. If you want to be the envy of your workmates, take the stew and potatoes to work in separate Tupperware and heat in the office microwave before assembling it in a mug to eat al desko. Beats a supermarket sandwich any day!

1 tablespoon olive oil

100g (3½oz) free-range cooking chorizo, sliced

1 small onion, finely chopped

700g (1lb 9oz) organic beef skirt, brisket or a decent stewing steak, cut into 3cm (1¼in) pieces

2 garlic cloves, sliced

1 tablespoon tomato purée

200ml (14fl oz) tomato passata

½ teaspoon smoked paprika

3 tablespoons Amontillado sherry

2 bay leaves

300ml (10fl oz) beef stock

400g (14oz) can butterbeans, drained

50g (1¾oz) green olives, pitted and sliced

a handful of chopped flat-leaf parsley

salt and freshly ground black pepper

FOR THE PATATAS BRAVAS-STYLE TOPPING

800g (1lb 12oz) potatoes, unpeeled and cut into 1.5cm (⅝in) cubes

2 tablespoons olive oil

1 teaspoon smoked paprika

To make the beef filling, heat the oil in a large, lidded pan, add the chorizo and onion and cook over a low heat for about 10 minutes until the onion is softened and the colour has run from the chorizo.

Tip in the beef and cook for a further 10 minutes, or until the beef is browned. Add the garlic, and salt and black pepper to taste.

Stir in the tomato purée, passata, smoked paprika, sherry, bay leaves and beef stock.

Bring to a simmer, then put the lid on the pan and cook over a low heat for 2 hours, or until the meat is tender, stirring from time to time. You may need to add a splash of water to loosen. You will get softer, more tender meat the longer you cook this, so leave it longer if you have the time or the inclination! The more you cook it, the more water will evaporate, so just keep adding a splash of water or stock to keep the right consistency.

Finally, add the butterbeans, green olives and parsley to the pan. Bring to a simmer and cook for a final 15 minutes. Taste and add any salt and pepper if you feel it needs it. Remove the bay leaves.

For the patatas bravas-style topping, preheat the oven to 220°C/200°C fan/425°F/gas mark 7. Toss the potatoes with the olive oil and arrange on a baking tray in a single layer. Roast for 20 minutes, then remove from the oven and top with the smoked paprika. Cook for a further 10–15 minutes, or until golden brown and crisp. Season with salt and pepper.

To serve, arrange the hot beef stew in whatever receptacle you would like to serve it in – it could be a pie dish (a 30cm/12in one would do the trick) or you could serve it in individual servings in a pot, mug, or even a jar that you've rescued from the recycling. Top with the hot patatas bravas-style topping and serve.

JACKFRUiT iS A GREAT PLANT-BASED REPLACEMENT FOR THE BEEF iN THiS RECiPE. USE 2 PORTiONS OF THE JACKFRUiT RECiPE ON PAGE 180.

JACK YOUR BODY

SMOKED MACKEREL HASH

You could eat this all day, every day, for breakfast, brunch, lunch and supper.
But as there are not 'plenty more fish in the sea' this dish is for once a month at most.
The easy onion pickle is a great go-to topping for many a rich saucy dish.

500g (1lb 2oz) undyed smoked mackerel

500ml (18fl oz) milk

a small bunch of flat-leaf parsley, stalks and leaves separated

a few sprigs of thyme

6 black peppercorns

1kg (2lb 4oz) Jersey Royal potatoes, cut into chunks

1 tablespoon olive oil

100g (3½oz) unsalted butter

2 medium onions, sliced

2 garlic cloves, finely chopped

25g (1oz) plain flour

5 tablespoons vermouth

1 teaspoon Dijon mustard

100g (3½oz) Parmesan, grated

1 tablespoon capers, drained

salt, to taste

a small handful of snipped chives, to garnish (optional)

FOR THE EASY RED ONION PICKLE

1 large red onion, very thinly sliced

120ml (4fl oz) cider vinegar

½ teaspoon caster sugar

1 tablespoon mustard seeds

1 teaspoon nigella seeds

freshly ground black pepper

To make the easy red onion pickle, put the onion, cider vinegar and sugar in a glass or ceramic bowl. Dry-fry the spices and add them to the mixture. Leave to marinate for at least 45 minutes, or preferably overnight. Give the pickle a stir from time to time to make sure everything is nicely coated in the vinegar, which will soften the onion.

For the mackerel hash, put the mackerel in a shallow pan, add enough milk to cover, plus the parsley stalks, thyme sprigs and peppercorns. Heat the pan and poach the mackerel for about 5 minutes. Strain, reserving 350ml (12fl oz) of the milk, discarding the parsley stalks, thyme and peppercorns. Flake the fish with a fork and set aside.

For the topping, cook the potatoes in a pan of boiling, salted water until just cooked, then drain.

Heat the olive oil and half of the butter in a large frying pan, add the onions and cook for about 15 minutes, or until tender and golden, stirring from time to time. Stir in the garlic and cook for a few minutes. Set aside.

Preheat the oven to 190°C/170°C fan/375°F/gas mark 5.

Heat 25g (1oz) butter in a pan, add the flour and cook until a biscuit-like aroma comes off the mixture. Gradually stir in the reserved milk, stirring constantly to make sure that the milk is absorbed by the roux. Pour in the vermouth and stir well, then mix in the mustard. Taste and add salt if needed. Remove from the heat and stir in the remaining 25g (1oz) of butter and 30g (1oz) of the Parmesan.

Put the cooked potatoes into a large bowl with the parsley leaves, cooked onions and any buttery juices from the pan.

Set aside a couple of tablespoons of the flaked fish, then mix together the remaining mackerel and the sauce in a large ovenproof dish, top with the potatoes and scatter over the remaining Parmesan. Bake for about 35 minutes, or until the topping is golden brown.

Just before serving, mix together the reserved flaked fish, capers and 2 tablespoons of the red onion pickle. Garnish the hash with the mackerel, caper and red onion mixture and top with snipped chives, if you like. Serve with more red onion pickle on the side, topped with freshly ground pepper.

CIAO!

WE'RE FANS OF BRISTOL-BASED APERITIVO'S LYON VERMOUTH, AND IT WOULD WORK WELL IN THIS RECIPE. (IT'S A VERY SIP-ABLE FRENCH-STYLE DRY VERMOUTH), BUT ANY DRY VERMOUTH CAN BE USED. OR YOU COULD ADD WHITE WINE AS AN ALTERNATIVE.

PULLED LAMB PIE

We've worked with the Campaign Against Living Miserably (CALM) who, like us, are strong believers in the power of a good chat. We find it's sometimes easier to talk about the 'heavy stuff' like how we're feeling when doing something else at the same time. So don't just invite your mates over to eat pie, get them round early to help you make it first. This pie's great for this as it takes a while to prepare, so there's plenty of time to talk it out.

2 brown onions, finely diced

4 celery sticks, finely diced

2 carrots, washed and finely diced

2 leeks, washed, split lengthways and cut into 2cm (¾in) chunks

1 garlic bulb, halved

2 bay leaves

6 sprigs of thyme

4 sprigs of rosemary, 2 whole, 2 picked

1 tablespoon organic rapeseed oil

1.5–2kg (3lb 5oz–4lb 8oz) lamb shoulder on the bone

3 garlic cloves, thinly sliced

250ml (9fl oz) white wine

800ml (1 ⅓ pints) hot lamb or chicken stock

2 x 400g (14oz) cans flageolet beans, drained

1 tablespoon white wine vinegar

juice of 1 lemon

1 tablespoon Dijon mustard

30g (1oz) flat-leaf parsley, coarsely chopped

salt and freshly ground black pepper

FOR THE TOPPING

1kg (2lb 4oz) waxy potatoes, thinly sliced (about 3mm/ ⅛in thick)

25g (1oz) butter

Preheat the oven to 180°C/160°C fan/350°F/gas mark 4.

Place the onions, celery, carrots, leeks, halved garlic bulb, bay leaves, thyme sprigs and two whole rosemary sprigs into a roasting dish, coat with the oil and mix to combine. Place the lamb shoulder on top, take a small sharp knife and make small incisions over the surface of the lamb. Stuff each hole with a slice of garlic and the rosemary leaves, then season the shoulder liberally with salt and pepper. Add the white wine and 300ml (10fl oz) of the hot stock to the dish, cover with foil and cook in the oven for 4 hours.

Remove from the oven and remove the foil (reserve for later) and increase the temperature to 220°C/200°C fan/425°F/gas mark 7. Baste the shoulder, add a splash more stock if the vegetables are drying out and return to the oven for 40 minutes–1 hour to brown the lamb and ensure the meat is tender and falling off the bone. Once browned, remove the lamb shoulder to a board and set aside.

Squeeze the roasted garlic cloves from their skins into the stock and vegetable mix, add the flageolet beans, white wine vinegar, lemon juice, Dijon mustard and parsley. Remove and discard the bay leaf.

Using two forks, shred the lamb shoulder into large chunks, discarding any bones and fatty bits. Add the meat to the bean mixture and stir to combine.

Arrange the sliced potatoes over the top of the mixture, in two or three layers, seasoning with salt and pepper in between each layer. Pour over the remaining stock, dot the butter over the top and place a layer of baking parchment on top, press down lightly and cover tightly with the reserved foil. Return to the oven and cook for 1 hour, then remove the foil and parchment and bake for a further 30 minutes until the potatoes are crisp and browned.

Serve with some steamed green or purple-sprouting broccoli if in season.

CROFTER'S PIE

This pie's best eaten by firelight while it's blowing a hooley outside. The swede and onion add some rooty depth to the buttery mash atop a rich and rustic game casserole. We're big believers in balancing meat content with a plant-based protein, so we've used white beans to do the job here. Now, where's the whisky...?

2 tablespoons organic rapeseed oil

6–8 venison sausages

2 brown onions, diced

2 celery sticks, diced

2 carrots, washed and diced

4 garlic cloves, crushed

2 bay leaves

4 sprigs of rosemary

2 star anise

1 teaspoon allspice

1 tablespoon tomato purée

250ml (9fl oz) red wine

500ml (18fl oz) game or beef stock

1 tablespoon Worcestershire sauce

400g (14oz) can chopped tomatoes

2 x 400g (14oz) cans white beans, such as cannellini, butter or haricot beans

200g (7oz) cavolo nero, stalks removed and leaves finely shredded

salt and freshly ground black pepper

FOR THE TOPPING

1 swede (500–600g/1lb 2oz–1lb 5oz), peeled and cut into 2cm (¾in) dice

1 brown onion, sliced

1kg (2lb 4oz) floury potatoes, cut into large chunks

100g (3½oz) unsalted butter

Preheat the oven to 180°C/160°C fan/350°F/gas mark 4.

Heat the oil in a heavy-based, shallow casserole over a medium–high heat and, when hot, brown the sausages. Remove from the pan and set aside.

Reduce the heat to medium and add the onions, celery and carrots to the pan, season with salt and pepper and cook for 10–15 minutes until beginning to caramelize, stirring occasionally. Add the garlic, bay leaves, rosemary sprigs, star anise and allspice and cook for a further 2 minutes, then stir through the tomato purée. Increase the heat, pour in the red wine and allow to bubble for 2 minutes. Add the stock, Worcestershire sauce and chopped tomatoes and bring the mixture to a simmer. Slice the venison sausages into 2cm (¾in) slices and add these and the white beans to the pan, place the lid on and cook in the oven for 1–1½ hours, checking and stirring every 20 minutes, and adding a splash of water if necessary.

Meanwhile, to make your clapshot topping, steam the swede and sliced onion until tender and boil the potatoes until cooked. Once both are ready, drain and mash together with the butter and season with salt and a generous amount of pepper. Set to one side.

Once your filling is thickened and ready, remove from the oven and increase the temperature to 200°C/180°C fan/400°F/gas mark 6. Stir the shredded cavolo nero through your filling. Transfer the filling to your pie dish and top with the clapshot mash, using a fork to spread this over the top and create ridges and furrows for crispy edges. Return to the oven and cook for 40 minutes–1 hour until golden and crispy on top.

GO PLANT BASED

YOU COULD EASILY MAKE THIS VEGAN BY SWITCHING THE SAUSAGES, STOCK AND BUTTER FOR YOUR FAVOURITE PLANT-BASED ALTERNATIVES.

THE BOTTOMLESS CRUNCH

There's no better way to kick off the weekend than with a long, leisurely bottomless brunch. That's bottomless coffee, smoothies or mimosas (we're not suggesting you cook without your pyjamas on for goodness sake!). Great served with poached eggs, beans or whatever tickles your weekend fancy.

1 tablespoon organic rapeseed oil, plus extra for drizzling

8 high-quality free-range pork sausages

200g (7oz) lardons

2 leeks, washed and cut into chunks

800g (1lb 12oz) floury potatoes

salt and freshly ground black pepper

FOR THE CHEESE SAUCE

50g (1¾oz) butter

50g (1¾oz) plain flour

500ml (18fl oz) milk

a few gratings of nutmeg

1 teaspoon English mustard

100g (3½oz) Somerset Cheddar, grated

Heat the oil in a wide, shallow ovenproof pan over a medium heat. Squeeze meatball-sized pieces of sausage meat out of the sausage skin into the pan. Cook so they brown on all sides, then add the lardons to the pan and brown. Tip in the leeks and toss in the fat, season and put on the lid. Cook for a further 6–8 minutes, stirring occasionally.

Meanwhile, grate the potatoes into a clean tea towel. Wrap the towel around the potato and, over the sink, squeeze out the excess water. Put into a bowl, season well and fork through until evenly distributed.

To make the cheese sauce, melt the butter in a saucepan and, when it's foaming, add the flour and cook over a medium heat, stirring continuously, for 3–4 minutes. Slowly add the milk, stirring with each addition. It may look lumpy at first but keep beating with a wooden spoon or whisk and it will become smooth. Once all the milk is added, keep stirring as it comes to a simmer. Add the nutmeg, mustard and cheese and season. Stir until everything is incorporated and the sauce is thick.

Preheat the oven to 200°C/180°C fan/400°F/gas mark 6.

Pour the cheese sauce over the sausage mixture, making sure it gets into all of the corners, then top with the grated potato and drizzle with a little oil. Cook for 30 minutes until the rösti top is browned and crispy around the edge and the sauce is bubbling.

PEAS & LOVE

To make it vegan, swap the sausage and lardons for your favourite plant-based alternatives and follow the plant-based béchamel sauce recipe on page 180.

WAFFLE BASKETS

Who doesn't love a pudding bowl you can eat? Especially when filled to the brim with all the sweet things you can imagine and slathered with sauce and sprinkles. Every big and little kid's dream.

125g (4½oz) plain flour
50g (1¾oz) cornflour
175g (6oz) icing sugar
½ teaspoon vanilla extract
a pinch of salt
200ml (7fl oz) water
1 tablespoon vegetable oil, plus extra for greasing

Mix the flours, icing sugar, oil and vanilla in a bowl, add a pinch of salt, then whisk in the water. Beat well until you have a smooth batter. Set aside in the fridge to rest for 2 hours.

When ready to cook, add a little oil to a non-stick pan and pour in about 4 tablespoons of batter. Swirl around the pan to create a thin even circle. Cook on both sides until golden, using a piece of kitchen paper to dry any moisture on the surface.

Once cooked, immediately drape inside a small bowl or pudding mould and carefully press a second smaller bowl over the waffle to make a basket shape. Leave to cool. Repeat with the remaining batter.

FILLING THE WAFFLE BASKETS IS ONLY LIMITED BY YOUR IMAGINATION; IN FACT, THE BIGGER, THE BETTER.

SEE PAGE 181 FOR OUR SIMPLE PLANT-BASED ICE CREAM RECIPE.

OUR FAVOURITE ICE CREAM PIE COMBOS ARE:

GLASTONBURY MUD PIE

CHOCOLATE ICE CREAM, SALTED CARAMEL SAUCE, CHOCOLATE SHAVINGS, TOASTED HAZELNUTS & TOPPED WITH A COOKIE OR BROWNIE

TOFFEE APPLE CRUMBLE PIE

VANILLA ICE CREAM, COOKED APPLES SPRINKLED WITH CRUSHED SHORTBREAD BISCUITS & DRIZZLED WITH TOFFEE SAUCE

LEMON MERINGUE PIE

FROZEN LEMON YOGURT, DOLLOPED WITH LEMON CURD & COVERED WITH SMASHED UP MERINGUES

TOFFEE PECAN PIE

TOFFEE ICE CREAM DRIZZLED WITH AGAVE SYRUP & TOPPED WITH TOASTED PECANS

WE'VE A GOT A BIT OF A BEEF

THE BAD

Beef is what you might call problematic...
but it doesn't have to be (more on that later).
First, let's look at why beef gets a bad rap.

- Current cattle systems generate high greenhouse gas emissions (20% of global food emissions come from cows alone). Even if you discount the methane cows produce, beef still comes out top of the highest emitters of CO_2.

- ...and it uses a lot of land, not just for the cows themselves but also to grow their feed. This is a massive issue, as by 2050 we'll have 60–70% more people to feed. So, the planet just isn't big enough to eat beef at the rate we do.

- ...and, as mentioned on page 30, there's the fact that demand for beef is driving the rapid increase in deforestation. We really need those trees!

- And what about the cows' welfare? Unfortunately, in some cases it can be pitifully low. Not surprising given that intensive beef farms are called 'Concentrated Animal Feeding Operations'. These CAFOs have been known to cause cows to suffocate from the inside out, as the diet is so unsuitable. They have no room to graze; instead they're left standing in their own waste, and they're pumped with antibiotics, which can drive resistant strains of bacteria in humans.

THE GOOD

But at the other end of the spectrum there is grass-fed beef, which actually has an important part to play in soil health and biodiversity. These pasture-reared cows not only lead far better lives, but their grazing also helps sequester huge amounts of carbon back into the soil.

But (and this is a big BUT) pasture-raised animals use far more land than CAFOs, and there just isn't enough space on the planet to produce enough of it to meet the current global demand for beef (we would need multiple planet Earths!). So, we must collectively reduce the amount of beef we eat, even if it's the 'good beef' kind.

Lucky for us in the UK, British beef farming has historically been pretty good – a large proportion of the UK and Irish beef is predominantly grass-fed. Therefore, we have a better chance than many of sourcing responsibly reared beef. However, it seems that CAFO-style meat production (it can't really be called farming!) is creeping into the UK, so watch out. A Union Jack on the packaging isn't enough of a guarantee anymore, so where you can, look out for labels such as Soil Association Organic, or Pasture for Life. Or ask your butcher yourself – if they're proud of the meat they supply they will be able to talk about the provenance of their beef till the cows come home!

DO THE PIE THING

So, IT COMES DOWN TO THIS:

- If you're eating beef, eat less of it less often. But buy the best that you can splash out on. Take time to cook it and savour every bite. Think of beef as a luxury for high days and holidays.

- Combine beef with other delicious proteins and vegetables – our Wild Farm Pudding (page 158) is a good example of this, where oysters and celeriac enhance both the taste and texture of the pudding while meaning the beef content can be reduced.

- Meat can often be replaced altogether without losing any of the flavour of a dish by using easy, everyday ingredients such as mushrooms. To test this theory, try The Reubeno on page 73. And the super-versatile roasted jackfruit on page 180 seems to satisfy even the most committed carnivore (Jon's son Ned still doesn't realize he's been eating meat-free jackfruit chilli for the past five years!)

NOT MANY PEOPLE KNOW THIS
BUT MOST OF THE WORLD'S OXYGEN
(ABOUT 70%) COMES FROM SEAWEED
AND OTHER MICROSCOPIC ALGAE.

NO TIN PIES

PATTIES, SLICES
& WONDERFULLY
SHAPED BAKES

DUCK PIE-THIVIER

This dainty dish looks like the old-fashioned sort that could house 24 blackbirds. In fact, we've used free-range confit duck, which is readily available nowadays.

320g (11½oz) packet ready-rolled puff pastry
1 free-range egg, lightly beaten
plain flour, for dusting

FOR THE FILLING

2 free-range duck confit legs
50ml (2fl oz) red wine
2 shallots, finely chopped
a few sprigs of thyme
70ml (2½fl oz) chicken stock
a handful of flat-leaf parsley, chopped
75g (2¾oz) membrillo paste
100g (3½oz) black pudding, crumbled
salt and freshly ground black pepper

BILL TO TAIL EATING

To make 'quackling', slice the reserved duck skin and arrange it on a baking tray. Roast in the oven for 10 minutes, or until nicely crisp. Drain the fat into a pan and put the duck skin on a plate. Salt the duck skin, to taste. Delicious sprinkled over a side of veg.

For the pie, heat the confit duck legs in a saucepan over a low heat to release the fat. If the confit contains plenty of fat in the can or packet, you can remove this from the pan to use for the next stage (or to add to roast potatoes!). Remove the duck from the pan.

Remove the skin from the duck legs and set it aside (see tip below). Using your hands – and it will get a bit messy! – pull away the duck meat to shred it, discarding any bones or gristle.

Heat a couple of tablespoons of the reserved duck fat in a saucepan – if the confit can or packet doesn't contain a lot of duck fat, you may need to add 1 tablespoon of oil instead.

Pour in the wine and cook to absorb the liquid, then tip in the shallots and thyme, and cook until the shallots are nicely softened.

Add the stock, tip in the shredded duck and cook for a few minutes. Add salt and pepper, to taste, and stir in the chopped parsley. Stir, remove the thyme sprigs, and then set aside to cool completely.

To assemble the pie, lightly flour your work surface and lay out the pastry on the floured surface, then cut out a disc using a plate as a guide; we used a 16cm (6¼in) diameter plate for this. Place the disc on a baking tray lined with greaseproof paper.

Spread the membrillo paste across the pastry disc, top with the crumbled black pudding and then pile the duck mixture on top. Put another piece of puff pastry over the whole thing to cover all the filling, and trim away any excess pastry to create an even round. Press around the edges to seal.

Brush the top with beaten egg, then make curved lines like spokes on the top of the pie, working from the centre outwards. Brush with more beaten egg. Leave the pie to chill in the fridge for at least 30 minutes before baking.

Preheat the oven to 220°C/200°C fan/425°F/gas mark 7.

Bake the pie in the oven for about 25 minutes, or until well-puffed and golden brown. Reduce the oven temperature to 180°C/160°C fan/350°F/gas mark 4 and bake for a further 20 minutes, taking care not to overbrown the pastry.

DROP & GROW
from LettUs Grow

'IT'S AEROPONIC! IT'S ULTRASONIC!'

IT'S A FARM IN A BOX!

Intensive farming doesn't have to be bad news for the planet, and LettUs Grow is a great example of this. They grow more food, with less resources, using aeroponics; growing plants in air and mist instead of soil. Like Great HoundTor on page 157, this method is regenerative; in this case recirculating water and nutrients back into the plants, which are also grown without any pesticides.

But this isn't the wilds of Dartmoor; it's slap-bang in the middle of an industrial estate in Bristol.

A LettUs Grow farm can fit into a shipping container and instead of a pretty farmhouse next door, you'll find a laboratory complete with scientists in white coats. This is vertical, indoor farming and it's part of the solution to the challenges we're facing as the world's population soars. Growing 'up' in this way and suspending plant roots in air instead of precious soil improves the amount of oxygen the plant gets, resulting in faster growth and higher yields, but in less space.

Aeroponic, indoor farming like this has been burgeoning for a while, but the team at LettUs Grow have taken the concept one step further, using ultrasonics to turn the nutrient-rich water into mist. Why? Because it means moisture can be distributed and controlled to the plant's exact requirements, so less water is needed, which combined with the faster growing times and scale-up possibilities, is an exciting prospect for the future of farming.

And as this magic happens indoors, these mini, but high-yield farms can be dropped in wherever there's a need for the produce grown, whatever the weather, climate and space available. So, for countries such as Norway or Qatar that fly in the majority of their fresh salad due to their climate, it massively reduces the air freight.

Fewer food miles, less embodied carbon, less cost.

WHY AEROPONICS WORK

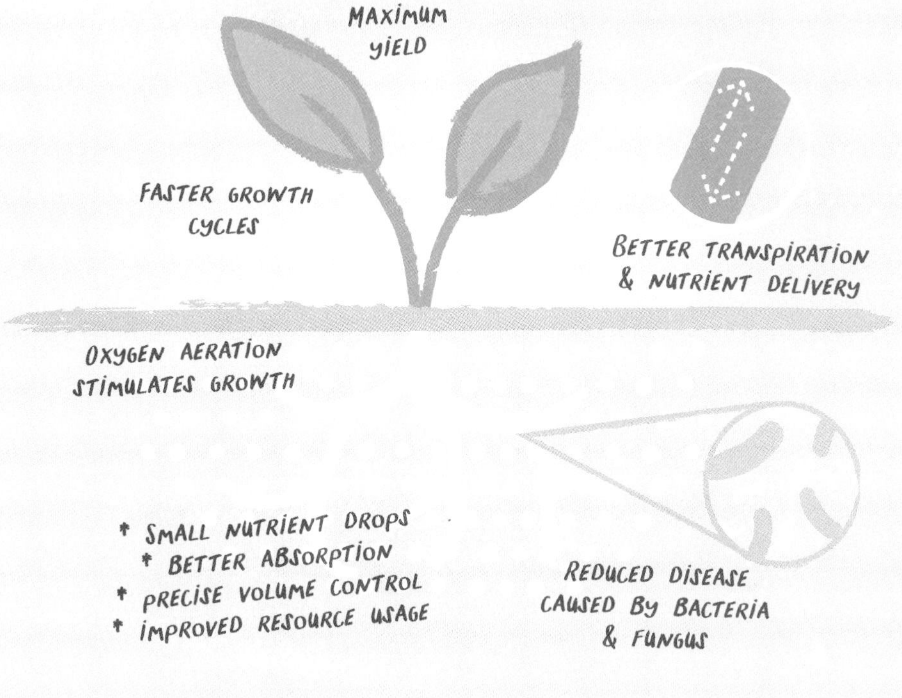

MAXIMUM YIELD

FASTER GROWTH CYCLES

BETTER TRANSPIRATION & NUTRIENT DELIVERY

OXYGEN AERATION STIMULATES GROWTH

* SMALL NUTRIENT DROPS
* BETTER ABSORPTION
* PRECISE VOLUME CONTROL
* IMPROVED RESOURCE USAGE

REDUCED DISEASE CAUSED BY BACTERIA & FUNGUS

MUSHROOM WWWELLINGTON

Take a moment to marvel at the superbly named Wood Wide Web, a wondrous 500-million-year-old social network of roots, fungi and bacteria, which lives under every forest floor, helping trees, plants (and therefore, us) flourish every day. This recipe is a respectful shout-out to all those mycorrhizal networks out there.

1 portion of rough puff pastry (page 26)

plain flour, for dusting

FOR THE FILLING

1 garlic bulb

4 tablespoons olive oil

300g (10½oz) spinach

2 shallots, very finely diced

6 garlic cloves, crushed

20g (¾oz) pine nuts

50g (1¾oz) panko breadcrumbs

2 tablespoons plant-based butter

zest and juice of 1 lemon

20g (¾oz) flat-leaf parsley, finely chopped

4 portobello mushrooms, sliced into thirds

100g (3½oz) garlic and herb plant-based cream cheese

2 tablespoons plant-based milk, plus extra fror glazing

salt and freshly ground black pepper

Preheat the oven to 200°C/180°C fan/400°F/gas mark 6.

Cut the top off the bulb of garlic, just exposing the tips of the cloves inside. Place the bulb in a small square of foil, drizzle with 1 tablespoon of the olive oil, season with salt and pepper, wrap up tightly and roast in the oven for 40 minutes. Remove from the oven and allow to cool.

Meanwhile, wash the spinach and place in a dry frying pan over a medium heat. Cook until wilted and then remove to a colander. Once cool enough to handle, transfer to a clean tea towel and squeeze out all the excess moisture. Roughly chop the spinach and set aside.

Place the same frying pan back over a medium heat, add 2 tablespoons of the oil and the shallots and cook for 5–10 minutes until beginning to caramelize. Add most of the crushed garlic and the pine nuts, season with salt and pepper and cook for a further 2 minutes until fragrant, then add the panko breadcrumbs, stirring continuously so that the crumbs don't scorch. Cook the mixture until the pine nuts are toasted and the breadcrumbs are golden – it should sound crunchy when stirred in the pan. Remove from the heat and spread in a thin layer on a plate to cool. Once cooled, mix with the chopped spinach and lemon zest.

Take the cooled garlic bulb, remove from the foil and squeeze out the garlic clove flesh into a small bowl. Add 1–2 teaspoons of lemon juice, season with salt and pepper to taste and set aside.

Place a frying pan over a high heat and add the remaining 2 tablespoonsof olive oil, then add the mushrooms and cook until beginning to brown. Add the plant-based butter and the remaining crushed garlic and cook for a further 2–4 minutes, continually basting the mushrooms in the garlic butter. Remove from the heat, stir through the chopped parsley and add 1 teaspoon of lemon juice.

Dust a work surface with flour and roll out the pastry to 3mm (⅛in) thick. Cut out four 12cm (4½in) circles and four 16cm (6¼in) circles. Place these on to two lined baking trays and return to the fridge to chill.

Spoon 1 tablespoon of spinach mixture into the centre of a 12cm (4½in) circle of pastry. Add three slices of mushroom, then spoon over another tablespoon of spinach mixture, plus a quarter of the roast garlic paste and a quarter of the cream cheese, creating a dome shape. Brush the edges of the pastry with plant-based milk and place a larger circle of pastry on top, shaping around the mushrooms to remove any air. Seal the edges by crimping or using a fork dipped in flour. Brush the top of the pie with more plant-based milk and then cut two slits in the top of each pie. Repeat with the remaining pastry circles and filling.

Bake in the oven for 20–25 minutes until golden, turning the tray for the last 5 minutes of cooking.

VELLY WELLY

A little bit more involved than most of the other recipes here, this will impress your friends, so it's well worth the effort. Traditionally, the meat and filling in a Beef Wellington was wrapped in a plain pancake to stop the pastry getting soggy. Here we've added flavoursome ingredients to the pancake itself.

½ **portion of rough puff pastry (page 26)**
plain flour, for dusting
1 free-range egg yolk

FOR THE PANCAKES

150ml (5fl oz) milk
20g (¾oz) dried porcini mushrooms
40g (1½oz) plain flour
1 free-range egg
4 black garlic cloves, finely chopped
olive oil, for frying
salt and freshly ground black pepper

FOR THE FILLING

700g (1lb 9oz) loin of wild venison
1 tablespoon organic rapeseed oil
wholegrain mustard, to serve

FOR THE STUFFING

1 teaspoon olive oil
100g (3½oz) baby leaf spinach
4 black garlic cloves, finely chopped

For the pancakes, warm the milk in a small pan. Add the dried mushrooms and leave for 10 minutes so that the milk absorbs all the lovely mushroomy flavours. Strain the milk, reserving the dried mushrooms for the stuffing.

Put the flour in a mixing bowl, whisk in the egg and then whisk in the milk to make a smooth batter. Transfer to the fridge to rest for 15 minutes – not too long as the porcini milk can thicken too much.

Just before you are ready to cook the pancakes, add the black garlic and some salt and pepper to taste.

To cook the pancakes, heat the olive oil in a pan and ladle some of the batter into the pan, tilting it to move the mixture around to make a thin, even layer. Cook the pancake for 1 minute on each side until golden brown. Carefully remove from the pan and set aside. Repeat to use up all the batter.

For the filling, preheat the oven to 200°C/180°C fan/400°F/gas mark 6. Season the venison with salt. Heat the oil in a pan and fry on all sides until browned all over. Then transfer to a roasting tin and cook for 5 minutes in the hot oven – give it another 3 minutes if you prefer the meat medium. Season with pepper and leave to cool.

For the stuffing, finely chop the reserved porcini mushrooms. Heat the olive oil in a pan, add the spinach, mushrooms and garlic and cook until the spinach has wilted. Leave to cool.

To assemble, roll the rough puff pastry into a rectangle large enough to enclose the venison and about 2mm (¹⁄₁₆in) thick. Place on to a piece of baking parchment, then cut the porcini pancakes large enough to wrap the venison and lay them on top of the pastry.

Spread the spinach over the porcini pancakes and then put the venison on top and fold the pancakes and pastry over to enclose the venison. Use wet fingers to seal the edges together, trim and brush with beaten egg. Place in the fridge and leave to rest for at least 30 minutes, or until you are ready to cook.

Preheat the oven to 220°C/200°C fan/425°F/gas mark 7.

Lightly score the Velly Welly with diagonal lines and brush with more beaten egg. Lightly oil a baking tray and place in the oven to get hot. Put the Velly Welly on the hot tray and bake for 30 minutes for medium-rare. Remove from the oven and leave to cool for 5 minutes before slicing. Serve with wholegrain mustard.

GREAT DANE!

A satisfying take on a classic 'Danish' filled here with peach, feta and oregano. The nutty brown butter pastry and salty feta offset the lush sweetness that comes from the roast peaches perfectly.

1 portion of brown butter pastry (page 19)

1 free-range egg, beaten

plain flour, for dusting

FOR THE FILLING

150g (5½oz) ricotta

100g (3½oz) feta, crumbled

2 teaspoons smoked salt, or to taste

1 tablespoon honey (local is always best)

6 sprigs of oregano, leaves picked from 4 sprigs and finely shredded

2 teaspoons sesame seeds

4 peaches, skinned, pitted and halved

In a bowl, whip the ricotta and feta together until thoroughly combined and fluffy, add a generous pinch of smoked salt to taste, 1 teaspoon of the honey and the shredded oregano.

Dust a work surface with flour and roll out the brown butter pastry to 3mm (⅛in) thick. Cut out eight 10cm (4in) squares and place on to two baking trays lined with baking parchment. Fold in a 1cm (½in) border of pastry around each edge of each pastry square and press down, then take each corner of pastry and twist it clockwise so that the folded corner now sits against the tray. Brush the edges of each pastry with beaten egg and sprinkle with sesame seeds.

Place 2–3 teaspoons of the ricotta and feta mixture into the middle of each pastry and spread across the base. Place the pies into the fridge to chill for 30 minutes.

Preheat the oven to 200°C/180°C fan/400°F/gas mark 6.

Remove the pies from the fridge and place a peach half on top of the whipped feta mix. Bake in the oven for 20–25 minutes until golden. Remove from the oven and drizzle each pie with some of the remaining honey, sprinkle with a small pinch of smoked salt and allow to cool on the baking tray for 5 minutes before removing to a wire rack to cool further. Sprinkle with oregano leaves from the remaining two stalks just before serving.

TOP TIP!

NECTARINES, FIGS OR PLUMS COULD BE USED IN PLACE OF PEACHES IF THEY ARE NOT IN SEASON.

BOURBON PULLED PORK PATTIES

The smoky barbecue flavours combined with the sweet, salty coating make these patties so moreish that you'll probably want to make double. Or conversely, use this cracking marinade for a pulled pork barbecue, then fill these patties with the leftovers. If not in season, switch the peaches for any other sweet fruit.

½ **portion of patty pastry (page 20)**

1 **free-range egg, beaten**

plain flour, for dusting

FOR THE FILLING

1kg (2lb 4oz) boneless, free-range, British pork shoulder

½ teaspoon organic rapeseed oil

2 peaches, sliced

1 onion, sliced

150ml (5fl oz) bourbon

150ml (5fl oz) apple juice

1 tablespoon white wine vinegar

2 teaspoons liquid smoke (optional)

2 tablespoons maple syrup

salt and freshly ground black pepper

FOR THE RUB

2 tablespoons molasses

1 tablespoon Worcestershire sauce

1 tablespoon smoked paprika

1 teaspoon chilli flakes

2 teaspoons mustard powder

2–3 sprigs of thyme, leaves picked

1 teaspoon garlic granules

In a small saucepan, warm all of the rub ingredients, stirring together until well combined.

Preheat the oven to 250°C/230°C fan/475°F/gas mark 9. Score the pork skin, dry with a piece of kitchen paper, then rub over the oil, and salt well. Put the peach and onion slices in the bottom of a small ovenproof dish and nestle the meat on top. Coat the meat (not the skin) with the wet rub. Pour the bourbon, apple juice, vinegar and liquid smoke (if using) into the bottom of the pan and crimp some foil around the sides of the pan, leaving the skin exposed but protecting the liquid from evaporating.

Cook for 25 minutes until the crackling is blistered and crisp. Reduce the temperature to 140°C/120°C fan/275°F/gas mark 1. Take the meat out of the oven and cover completely with foil, making a tent shape so it doesn't stick to the crackling. Cook for 3 hours until the meat is falling apart.

Increase the oven temperature to 250°C/230°C fan/475°F/gas mark 9, remove the foil from the pan and re-crisp the crackling for 10 minutes. Remove from the oven and reduce the temperature to 220°C/200°C fan/400°F/gas mark 6.

Remove the crackling and set aside. Remove the meat from the pan and use two forks to pull it apart, discarding the fat. Pour the onions, peaches and cooking liquor into a saucepan and boil for 5–10 minutes until the sauce is reduced and thick. Tip this into the shredded meat and stir well. Taste and season, then set aside to cool.

Dust a work surface with flour and roll out the patty pastry to 3mm (⅛in) thick. Cut out eight circles about 15cm (6in) wide; we use a side plate to cut around. Spoon the mixture on to the bottom half of each circle, leaving a 2cm (¾in) border clear around the edge. Brush the edge with the beaten egg, then fold the top half over the filling and press the edges together with a fork.

Put the patties on a baking tray and brush the tops with beaten egg. Let rest for 5 minutes, then bake for 20 minutes until golden brown.

While the patties are cooking, scrape any fat from the inside of the crackling, then chop the crackling finely. Mix with the maple syrup and when the patties come out of the oven, brush them with the maple crackling mix.

JACKFRUIT IS A GREAT PLANT-BASED REPLACEMENT FOR THE BEEF IN THIS RECIPE. USE 2½ PORTIONS OF THE JACKFRUIT RECIPE ON PAGE 180.

CHANA-RAMA PATTIES

The most loved recipe from our patty range, this had to be in the book! Chana is basically half a chickpea, dried. And we can't praise these unassuming little lentils highly enough. So humble yet so mighty, they're a superfood in every sense of the word: packed with health benefits, super sustainable, cheap and delicious. And ridiculously versatile. We recommend you make extra filling to have for breakfast, lunch, dinner – just top with crispy fried onions and herbs.

1 portion of patty pastry (page 20)

2 tablespoons plant-based milk

FOR THE FILLING

2 tablespoons organic rapeseed oil

1 large brown onion, diced

3 tablespoons Madras curry paste

2 tablespoons tomato purée

100g (3½oz) split red lentils, thoroughly rinsed in water until it runs clear, then cooked in boiling water for 20 minutes

100g (3½oz) yellow split peas (chana dal), thoroughly rinsed in water until it runs clear, then cooked in boiling water for 20 minutes

1 small sweet potato, peeled and chopped into 2cm (¾in) dice

500ml (18fl oz) vegetable stock

400g (14oz) can chickpeas, drained and rinsed

200g (7oz) spinach

20g (¾oz) coriander, stalks finely chopped, leaves roughly chopped

juice of ½ lemon

1 teaspoon black mustard seeds

1 teaspoon nigella seeds

TO SERVE

3 tablespoons mango chutney or lime pickle

6 tablespoons plant-based yogurt

Heat the oil in a heavy-based casserole dish over a medium heat and, when hot, add the onion and cook for 10 minutes until golden and caramelized. Add the Madras curry paste and tomato purée and cook for a further 2 minutes until fragrant. Add the drained, cooked lentils and split peas and the sweet potato, followed by the vegetable stock, bring to a simmer and cook for 40 minutes–1 hour until the peas and lentils are tender.

Add the chickpeas and cook for a further 20–40 minutes until the potato is cooked and the peas and lentils have formed a thick sauce. Add the spinach and finely chopped coriander stalks, stir to combine and then remove from the heat to cool completely once the spinach has wilted. Once cool, stir through the chopped coriander leaves and lemon juice.

Dust a work surface with flour and roll out the patty pastry to 3mm (⅛in) thick. Cut out eight circles 12cm (4½in) wide and place on to two lined baking trays. Spoon 3 tablespoons of the cooled filling on to the bottom half of each circle, leaving a 2cm (¾in) border around the edge. Brush the edges with a little plant-based milk and fold the top half of the circle over the filling to form a semicircle. Use a fork dusted in flour to seal the edges. Place the patties in the fridge to chill for 30 minutes.

Meanwhile, preheat the oven to 180°C/160°C fan/350°F/gas mark 4.

Remove from the fridge and brush the surface of each patty with some plant-based milk, sprinkle each patty with some mustard and nigella seeds. Bake in the oven for 20–25 minutes until golden.

Serve with mango chutney or lime pickle swirled through some plant-based yogurt.

TOP TIP! IF YOU DON'T HAVE MUSTARD OR NIGELLA SEEDS, YOU CAN USE WHOLE CUMIN SEEDS OR SESAME SEEDS IN THEIR PLACE.

HOLY CHIPOTLE PATTIES

Don't want to blow our own trumpets, but these are like a Mariachi band for the mouth. Feel free to freestyle with the filling (after all, this is our riff on a Mexican chilli) – it's great for using up leftovers and you can dial up the heat with some extra chillies as you like.

1 portion of patty pastry (page 20)

olive oil, for brushing

plain flour, for dusting

FOR THE FILLING

1–2 chipotle chillies, to taste

100ml (3½fl oz) just-boiled water

1 teaspoon cumin seeds

1 teaspoon mustard seeds

1 tablespoon vegetable oil

1 onion, diced

350g (12oz) sweet potato, diced (peeled or scrubbed)

½ teaspoon vegetable bouillon

2 teaspoons tomato purée

400g (14oz) can black beans, rinsed and drained

2 tablespoons canned sweetcorn

juice of ½ lime

a small handful of chopped coriander

1 teaspoon smoked paprika

salt and freshly ground black pepper

Soak the chillies in the just-boiled water for 20 minutes. Dry-fry the cumin and mustard seeds in a hot pan.

Heat the oil in a separate pan and fry the onion until softened – for at least 10 minutes.

Add the sweet potatoes to the pan. Drain the liquid from the chillies into a measuring jug and add enough water to measure 200ml (7fl oz) in total. Mix in the bouillon powder. Chop the soaked chillies.

Add the tomato purée to the pan, mix in, then add the bouillon liquid and the black beans. Stir in the chopped chilli and toasted cumin and mustard seeds. Cook for 10 minutes, or until the liquid is absorbed and the potatoes are tender. Stir in the sweetcorn and lime juice. Set aside and leave to cool. Add the chopped coriander and mix together.

Preheat the oven to 180°C/160°C fan/350°F/gas mark 4 and line a baking tray with baking parchment.

Dust a work surface with flour and roll out the pastry. Cut out eight 16cm (6¼in) wide circles and brush the edges with olive oil – use the edge of a plate as a guide. Put about 3 tablespoons of the filling into the centre of each of the circles and fold in half, using your fingers to crimp the pastry. You could also use a pasty mould to do this.

Lay the patties on the prepared tray, brush with olive oil and sprinkle with paprika. Bake for 30 minutes, checking after 20 minutes. Serve hot or cold.

IF YOU DO WANT TO PEEL THE POTATOES FOR THESE PATTIES, THE PEELINGS MAKE A GREAT SNACK (YES, REALLY). PUT THE PEEL ON A BAKING TRAY, DRIZZLE IN A LITTLE OIL AND ROAST IN THE OVEN WHILE THE PATTIES ARE COOKING. THEY WILL TAKE ABOUT 10 MINUTES BUT CHECK AFTER 5 MINUTES. SPRINKLE WITH SALT AND A LITTLE SMOKED PAPRIKA TO SERVE.

FAKE MOOS ROVERS

This is a riff on our legendary plant-based 'steak' recipe which we usually make with deforestation-free jackfruit and cracked green peppercorns. Here we've switched the stout out for brandy and added loads of caramelized onions, a glug of oat cream and a splash of vegan Worcestershire sauce.

1 portion of vegan suet pastry (page 28)

plain flour, for dusting

FOR THE FILLING

1kg (2lb 4oz) canned jackfruit, drained

3 teaspoons vegetable bouillon

2 tablespoons olive oil, plus extra for brushing and greasing

4 onions, sliced

1 heaped teaspoon chopped rosemary

2 garlic cloves, finely chopped

2 tablespoons balsamic vinegar

50g (1¾oz) soft light brown sugar

3 tablespoons brandy

1 teaspoon green peppercorns, cracked, plus extra for the topping

1 tablespoon vegan Worcestershire sauce, plus extra, to taste

200ml (7fl oz) oat cream

salt and freshly ground black pepper

Preheat the oven to 200°C/180°C fan/400°F/gas mark 6. Grease two baking trays with oil, then place in the oven to heat.

Pat the jackfruit dry using a clean tea towel or kitchen paper. Tip the jackfruit into a bowl and sprinkle over the vegetable bouillon. Stir to coat the fruit in the powder. Tip the jackfruit on to the preheated trays and cook for 20 minutes, checking after 15 minutes and turning over halfway through.

Heat the oil in a pan and cook the sliced onions over a low heat for about 30 minutes, stirring regularly, until nicely soft and starting to caramelize. Add the rosemary and garlic and cook for a few more minutes.

Stir in the vinegar, sugar and brandy, and continue to cook until the mixture resembles an onion marmalade – the liquid will have reduced, and the onions will have become dark and sticky – this will take about another 20–30 minutes.

Add the green peppercorns, then 100ml (3½fl oz) water and the Worcestershire sauce. Cook so that the onions absorb the liquid slightly, then stir in the jackfruit and then the oat cream, taking care not to let it boil once the cream has been added. Taste and add salt and pepper, plus more Worcestershire sauce if liked. Set aside and leave to cool.

When you are ready to assemble the rovers, dust a work surface with flour and roll out the pastry until about 3mm (⅛in) thick. Cut out eight rectangles measuring 15 x 7cm (6 x 2¾in) for the bases. Cut another eight rectangles, slightly larger, for lids. Lay the bases on a lined baking sheet and brush the edges with water, then pile an eighth of the filling on to each base. Gently place the lids over the top of the filling and press down the edges to seal.

Combine a generous pinch of the peppercorns in a bowl with a dash of olive oil. Brush the rovers with the peppercorn oil. Make a couple of small holes in the centre of each rover to let out steam, and place in the fridge for at least 20 minutes.

Bake the rovers in the oven for 35–40 minutes, or until golden brown.

THAI CHOOK ROVERS

We discontinued our Thai Chook Pie a few years ago and have been inundated
with requests to bring it back ever since. Until that happens, here's the recipe,
in all its zingy, green curry glory.

**1 portion of suet pastry
(page 28)**

1 free-range egg, beaten

plain flour, for dusting

FOR THE FILLING

2 tablespoons Thai green
curry paste

400ml (14fl oz) coconut milk

2 teaspoons light soy sauce

500g (1lb 2oz) skinless, boneless
free-range chicken thigh fillets,
cut into 2cm (¾in) pieces

2 teaspoons organic rapeseed oil

1 onion, diced

3 garlic cloves, crushed

1cm (½in) piece of fresh ginger,
grated

2 hot red chillies, deseeded
and finely chopped

50g (1¾oz) creamed coconut,
grated

200g (7oz) sweet potato, peeled
and cut into 1cm (½in) dice

1 teaspoon chilli flakes

salt and freshly ground
black pepper

FOR THE SWEET CHILLI
CRÈME FRAÎCHE

200g (7oz) crème fraîche

3 tablespoons sweet chilli sauce

Combine the Thai green curry paste, 3 tablespoons of the coconut milk
and the soy sauce in a large bowl. Add the chicken pieces and use your
hands to massage the marinade into the chicken. Cover and refrigerate
for at least 30 minutes.

Heat the oil in a large pan and gently cook the onion for 5 minutes,
then add the garlic, ginger and chillies. Increase the heat to medium,
add the marinated chicken and cook for 10 minutes.

Pour over the remaining coconut milk, stir in the creamed coconut
and season. Bring to a simmer, add the sweet potato and cook for
10 minutes until the sauce is thick and the potato has softened. Set
aside to cool.

When you are ready to assemble the rovers, dust a work surface with
flour and roll out the pastry until about 3mm (⅛in) thick. Cut out eight
rectangles measuring 15 x 7cm (6 x 2¾in) for the bases. Cut another
eight rectangles, slightly larger, for lids. Lay the bases on a lined baking
sheet and brush the edges with beaten egg, then pile an eighth of the
filling on to each base. Gently place the lids over the top of the filling
and press down the edges to seal. Brush with more beaten egg and
sprinkle with chilli flakes. Make a couple of small holes in the centre
of each rover to let out steam, and place in the fridge for at least
20 minutes.

Preheat the oven to 200°C/180°C fan/400°F/gas mark 6.

Bake the rovers in the oven for 30–35 minutes, or until golden brown.
Mix together the crème fraîche and sweet chilli sauce and serve as
a dip alongside.

FARM FACT

CHEAP MEAT COMES AT THE EXPENSE OF THE FARM
ANIMALS THEMSELVES. ALWAYS CHOOSE FREE-RANGE
OR ORGANIC CHICKEN TO ENSURE YOU'RE SUPPORTING
FARMERS WITH THE HIGHEST WELFARE STANDARDS.

RUBY ROVERS

Classic buttered chicken in a portable pie with a bit of lime pickle stirred into the filling. A crowd-pleaser if ever there was one. Brush the pastry with garlic and coriander butter when it comes out of the oven, garlic naan-style.

1 portion of suet pastry (page 28)

1 free-range egg, beaten

plain flour, for dusting

FOR THE FILLING

700g (1lb 9oz) skinless, boneless free-range chicken thigh fillets, cut into 2cm (¾in) pieces

2 tablespoons lemon juice

½ teaspoon salt

½ teaspoon chilli powder

1 teaspoon ground paprika

1 teaspoon ground cumin

1 teaspoon garam masala

290g (10¼oz) natural yogurt

2 tablespoons ghee or clarified butter

2 onions, diced

2 garlic cloves, crushed to a paste

4cm (1½in) piece of fresh ginger, crushed to a paste

2 large red peppers, deseeded and diced

1 tablespoon tomato purée

½ teaspoon ground turmeric

1 teaspoon ground fenugreek

a generous pinch of demerara sugar

a small handful of coriander, roughly chopped

80g (2¾oz) lime pickle

FOR THE GARLIC & CORIANDER BUTTER

2 tablespoons ghee or clarified butter

3 garlic cloves, finely sliced

1 tablespoon chopped coriander

For the filling, place the chicken in a bowl and cover in the lemon juice and salt. Add the chilli powder, paprika, cumin, garam masala and 150g (5½oz) of the yogurt and mix well. Cover and set aside to marinate in the fridge for at least 30 minutes, or overnight if you have time.

To finish the chicken, preheat the oven to 200°C/180°C fan/400°F/gas mark 6 and line a baking tray with baking parchment. Tip the chicken on to the tray in one layer and cook for 17 minutes. Once cooked, set aside and reserve the cooking juices.

Heat the ghee or clarified butter in a large pan and fry the onions until softened. Add the garlic, ginger and red peppers and fry for a few more minutes. Stir in the tomato purée and the reserved cooking juices from the chicken, add the turmeric and fenugreek and cook for another minute until nicely aromatic. Reduce the heat and add the marinated chicken, the remaining 140g (5oz) of yogurt and the sugar. Cook for another minute, not allowing it to come to the boil. Remove from the heat, leave to cool and then stir in the coriander and lime pickle.

When you are ready to assemble the rovers, dust a work surface with flour and roll out the pastry until about 3mm (⅛in) thick. Cut out eight rectangles measuring 15 x 7cm (6 x 2¾in) for the bases. Cut another eight rectangles, slightly larger, for lids. Lay the bases on a lined baking sheet and brush the edges with beaten egg, then pile an eighth of the filling on to each base. Gently place the lids over the top of the filling and press down the edges to seal. Make a couple of small holes in the centre of each rover to let out steam, and place in the fridge for at least 20 minutes.

Preheat the oven to 200°C/180°C fan/400°F/gas mark 6 while the rovers are chilling. Bake them in the oven for 30–35 minutes, or until golden brown.

For the garlic and coriander butter, melt the ghee or clarified butter in a small pan and add the finely sliced garlic. Lightly fry until aromatic. Remove from the heat, add the chopped coriander and set aside.

When the rovers are baked, brush the top of each one with the garlic and coriander butter. Serve the pies hot or cold.

ODE TO TROUT

Digby Trout was a good fun man with a good fun name who took a punt on Pieminister, helping us hugely in the early days. This pie's a bow to him and a bow to Eastern Europe with a coulibiac-style pie made using wild trout, wild rice, sour cherries and dill.

½ **portion of sourdough pastry (page 25)**

plain flour, for dusting

1 tablespoon melted butter

1 tablespoon milk

FOR THE FILLING

400g (14oz) wild trout fillets

2 tablespoons olive oil

1 onion, finely chopped

1 garlic clove, finely chopped

150g (5½oz) basmati and wild rice mixture

300ml (10fl oz) fish stock

150ml (5fl oz) white wine

a small handful of chopped flat-leaf parsley

1 tablespoon chopped dill

zest of 1 lemon and juice of ½

70g (2½oz) dried sour cherries

salt and freshly ground black pepper

FOR THE SALAD

½ cucumber, thinly sliced

¼ onion, thinly sliced

½ teaspoon salt

1 tablespoon chopped dill, plus extra to garnish

1 tablespoon white wine vinegar

100g (3½oz) soured cream

Heat the grill to hot, brush the trout fillets with 1 tablespoon of the oil and grill for 5 minutes on each side. Remove the skin (if on), flake the flesh and remove any bones. Set aside.

In a pan, heat the remaining tablespoon of olive oil, add the onion, garlic and rice and cook over a low heat for a couple of minutes. Add the fish stock and wine, cover with a lid wrapped in a tea towel and cook for about 15 minutes until most of the liquid has been absorbed and the rice is cooked. Add the chopped parsley, dill, lemon zest and juice, and plenty of salt and pepper. Leave to cool.

Line a baking tray with baking parchment. Make a fish-shaped template out of paper. Dust a work surface with flour, then roll out half the sourdough pastry into a large rectangle that will fit on your baking tray. Cut around the fish template and transfer the fish-shaped pastry to the baking tray. Spread the flaked trout down the middle of the pastry fish, leaving space around the edge. Top with the rice mixture, shaping it so that it is rounded at the top. Finish with the sour cherries as a final layer on the top.

Roll out the remaining pastry and use the fish template to cut out a pastry fish that is 2cm (¾in) wider than the base. Moisten the edge of the pastry base with a little water, then carefully lift the larger fish lid over the top to encase the filling. Press the edges together to seal and then crimp the edges. You can now add some fish markings to your lid if you like. Place in the fridge for at least 30 minutes before baking.

For the salad, pat the cucumber dry using a clean tea towel to remove any moisture and put the cucumber and onion in a bowl with the salt and dill. Mix together the vinegar and soured cream in a separate bowl, and then combine with the cucumber and onion. Cover and leave to chill in the fridge for about 1 hour. Season with black pepper and more dill to garnish.

Combine the melted butter and milk in a small bowl. Brush the pie with the butter mixture to make a glaze.

To finish the pie, preheat the oven to 200°C/180°C fan/400°F/gas mark 6. Bake the pie for about 30 minutes, or until the pastry is golden brown. If it starts to go too brown, simply cover with a sheet of foil. Serve hot or cold in slices with the cucumber salad.

ECO POINTS

WILD FISH, SUSTAINABLY CAUGHT, IS OFTEN THE BEST OPTION. BUT IF YOU CAN ONLY FIND FARMED FISH, RAINBOW TROUT IS ONE OF THE MORE SUSTAINABLE OPTIONS; THEY'RE FARMED IN PONDS WHICH HAVE A FAR LOWER ENVIRONMENTAL IMPACT THAN FISH FARMED IN OPEN NET PENS.

TUTTI FRUTTI ROLY POLY

'Tutti Frutti' literally means 'all the fruits' in Italian, and this recipe is dedicated to anyone who has a sticky selection of nearly finished jams at the back of the cupboard (that's everyone, right?!). Now's your chance to go 'full tutti frutti' and use 'em all up in one go.

200g (7oz) plain flour, plus extra for dusting

1 teaspoon bicarbonate of soda

50g (1¾oz) butter or plant-based butter, cold, plus extra for greasing

50g (1¾oz) vegetable suet

80–100ml (2½–3½fl oz) dairy milk or oat milk

vegetable oil, for greasing (optional)

100g (3½oz) jam (use up any odds and ends you have)

Put the flour and bicarb in a large bowl, then rub in the butter with your fingertips until there are no lumps. Stir in the suet, then make a well in the centre of the flour mix and add the milk. Using a table knife, make a cutting motion through the mixture to start to combine the milk and dry ingredients. As it starts to come together, use your hands to bring it into a ball of dough. Cover in reusable wrap and refrigerate for 30 minutes.

While the dough is resting, make your steaming set-up. Preheat the oven to 180°C/160°C fan/350°F/gas mark 4. Put two shelves, one above the other in the oven. Set a large roasting tin on the lower shelf, carefully fill with boiling water from the kettle and steadily slide the shelf back in.

Lay a 40cm (16in) long sheet of foil on a work surface and place the same size greaseproof paper on top. Grease well with a little extra butter or thin covering of vegetable oil.

Remove the dough from the fridge and dust a work surface with flour. Pat out the pastry into a rough square, then roll out into a 20cm (8in) square. Spread over the jam, leaving a 2cm (¾in) gap at one edge. If using several jams, you can mix them or apply them in stripes.

Roll up the dough like a Swiss roll, ending at the jam-less edge. Press the seam together to seal, then carefully lift the roly-poly on to the middle of the greaseproof paper, seam-side down. Use a long palette knife or cake lifter to help.

Gather the greaseproof paper and foil up around the roly-poly and crimp the edges together to seal in the steam it creates. Leave plenty of space for the dough to expand.

Carefully transfer the foil parcel to the upper shelf in the oven and cook for 1 hour. Once cooked, lift out of the oven, taking care to avoid the hot steam. Leave to sit in its foil parcel for 5 minutes before carefully unwrapping. Serve in thick slices, hot, with custard.

THIS GOES PERFECTLY WITH OUR PLANT-BASED CUSTARD ON PAGE 181.

DON'T BELIEVE THE HYPE

PLASTICS, BIO PLASTICS AND ASSOCIATED GREEN WASHING IS A GROWING PROBLEM IN FOOD PRODUCTION.

You've heard the stats:

By the year 2050 there will be more plastic in our oceans than fish (by weight).

The world has produced over 9 billion tonnes of plastic since the 1950s.

Only 9% of all plastic ever produced has been properly recycled.

There are 13 times more pieces of plastic in our oceans than stars in our galaxy.

Recently there's been a lot of talk about new compostable materials to replace plastics, also known as bioplastics. But we know from first-hand experience that these are sometimes not the wonder materials we've been led to believe they are...

A few years ago, we thought we'd replace the plastic windows on our pie box fronts with a compostable alternative made from wood pulp. It seemed like the answer to our prayers. But it soon became clear that these 'compostable plastics' need very specific conditions to break down and end up either contaminating food waste streams if put in a domestic food waste bin (the machinery treats it like plastic) or if they make it to landfill the absence of oxygen means they often break down, releasing methane and carbon dioxide into the atmosphere and toxic leachate into waterways.

Until our recycling infrastructures have the capability to process these bioplastics, there is no safe place for them to go. So, unlike us, don't be fooled!

This taught us that the best thing we can do as a manufacturer is simplify our packaging. That's why we replaced our box windows with a pie photo instead. Turns out the windows weren't as important as we thought.

DO THE PIE THING

WHAT CAN WE DO AS CONSUMERS?

- Don't wish-cycle. Check you are clear on which materials can be recycled and how in your area – beware of greenwashing on packaging, even by well-meaning businesses.

- Lobby your local waste provider to improve the kerbside service they provide; demand more clarification over what materials they can take (and where they take them!)

- Audit your recycling box – is there something you buy a lot of that you could start buying in a different way, like using refill shops where you take your own containers, to reduce the amount of packaging waste you generate. Just one change like this every few months makes a difference.

How quickly plastic decomposes in the sea

CIGARETTE BUTT 20 YEARS

PLASTIC BAG 20 YEARS

STYROFOAM CUP 50 YEARS

CAN HOLDER 400 YEARS

PLASTIC BOTTLE 450 YEARS

DISPOSABLE NAPPIES 450 YEARS

FISHING LINE 600 YEARS

PIE DISH PIES

BIG PIES, PARTY PIES,
FAMILY FAVOURITES &
OTHER COMFORT FOOD

THE BIG NIGHT TIMPANO

In 2015, as fans of the film *Big Night*, we entered our version of a Timpano pie into the British Pie Awards. It won Gold, and for good reason: it's one of the greatest celebration pies ever invented. It takes time and dedication to make one – you'll need to clear the diary for a couple of days but it's worth it. Make all the elements on day one, then build the pie on day two.

1 portion of shortcrust pastry (page 27)

plain flour, for dusting

FOR THE FILLING

6 Italian-style sausages

olive oil, for frying

200g (7oz) chard, stalks discarded

1 teaspoon garlic granules

500g (1lb 2oz) ricotta

7 eggs, 1 beaten

¼ nutmeg, grated

140g (5oz) penne pasta, cooked

250g (9oz) salami, chopped

50g (1¾oz) Pecorino Romano, grated

FOR THE RAGÙ

500ml (18fl oz) just-boiled water

25g (1oz) porcini mushrooms

1 tablespoon olive oil

1 onion, finely diced

2 carrots, washed and finely diced

2 celery sticks, finely diced

2 garlic cloves, crushed

200g (7oz) Puy lentils, rinsed and drained

1 tablespoon tomato purée

200ml (7fl oz) red wine

500ml (18fl oz) passata

a small bunch of thyme, leaves picked

a small bunch of oregano, leaves picked and chopped

1 bay leaf

salt and freshly ground black pepper

In a bowl, pour the just-boiled water over the porcini and leave to steep for 30 minutes.

Heat the oil for the ragù in a large heavy-based saucepan and gently cook the onion, carrots and celery for 8–10 minutes before adding the garlic. Drain the porcini, reserving the liquor and chop the mushrooms. Add the mushrooms and lentils to the pan and stir in the tomato purée, red wine, passata and half the mushroom liquor. Add the herbs to the pan and season well. Bring to a simmer and leave to cook for 1 hour. Add more of the mushroom liquor if the ragù gets too thick.

Squeeze the sausage meat out of the skins to make small meatballs. Heat a frying pan with a little oil and fry the meatballs on all sides. Remove from the pan with a slotted spoon, then add the chard and garlic granules to the pan, season well and toss in the oil until the chard starts to wilt. Remove and set aside.

In another bowl, mix together the ricotta, beaten egg, nutmeg, and some salt and pepper until well combined.

Cook the eggs for 6 minutes in boiling water, cool in cold water, then peel off the shells. Set aside.

When the ragù is ready, discard the bay leaf and spoon some over the cooked pasta, enough to coat it well. Set aside to cool.

Preheat the oven to 180°C/160°C fan/350°F/gas mark 4.

When you're ready to construct the pie, dust a work surface with flour and roll out the pastry to 3mm (⅛in) thick and large enough to line and cover a cast-iron pan; ours is 25cm (10in) in diameter. Place a circle of greaseproof paper in the bottom of the pan and grease the sides with oil. Carefully line the pan with the pastry. Leave it draping over the edges of the pan so you can fold it over the top once filled.

Spoon in the pasta and spread out evenly. Next, thinly spread over half of the ricotta mixture, then scatter with the salami and the chard. Nestle in the eggs and meatballs together on the next layer and sprinkle with the Pecorino. Cover with the remaining ragù and the last of the ricotta. Fold the edges of the pastry over the top of the pie, using offcuts to cover any gaps. Put the lid on the pan and cook for 1 hour, then remove the lid and cook for a further 20 minutes until the top is golden.

Allow the pie to cool in the pan for 20 minutes. Use a palette knife to loosen the sides of the pie before carefully inverting it on to a serving plate or board. Leave to cool for another 10 minutes before cutting. Serve with a big green salad and a large glass of red.

BIG PLANT-BASED TIMPANO

Because why should meat eaters be the only ones to celebrate with a Timpano pie? Like the original meat version, this is probably best constructed over two days. Make all of the elements on day one, then leave to cool overnight and construct the following day.

1 portion of vegan shortcrust pastry (page 27)

plain flour, for dusting

FOR THE FILLING

200g (7oz) butternut squash, peeled and chopped into 1cm (½in) cubes

2 tablespoons olive oil

1 teaspoon dried sage

1 teaspoon chilli flakes

6 plant-based sausages

250g (9oz) chard, thick stalks discarded

1 teaspoon garlic granules

140g (5oz) penne pasta, cooked al dente

1 portion of plant-based béchamel (page 180)

100g (3½oz) plant-based Parmesan, grated

FOR THE RAGÙ

500ml (18fl oz) just-boiled water

25g (1oz) porcini mushrooms

1 tablespoon olive oil

1 onion, finely diced

2 carrots, washed and finely diced

2 celery sticks, finely diced

2 garlic cloves, crushed

200g (7oz) Puy lentils, rinsed and drained

1 tablespoon tomato purée

250ml (9fl oz) red wine (vegan)

500ml (18fl oz) passata

a small bunch of thyme, leaves picked

a small bunch of oregano, leaves picked and chopped

2 bay leaves

In a bowl, pour the just-boiled water over the porcini and leave to steep for 30 minutes.

Heat the oil for the ragù in a large heavy-based saucepan and gently cook the onion, carrots and celery for 8–10 minutes before adding the garlic. Drain the porcini, reserving the liquor and chop the mushrooms. Add the mushrooms and lentils to the pan and stir in the tomato purée, red wine, passata and half the mushroom liquor. Add the herbs to the pan and season well. Bring to a simmer and leave to cook for 1 hour. Add more of the mushroom liquor if the ragù gets too thick.

Preheat the oven to 180°C/160°C fan/350°F/gas mark 4.

Toss the butternut squash in some of the oil, the sage and chilli and some salt and pepper. Roast for 15 minutes, then set aside to cool.

Cut the sausages into bite-sized chunks. Heat a frying pan with a little oil and fry on all sides. Remove from the pan with a slotted spoon, then add the chopped chard and garlic granules, season well and toss in the oil until the chard starts to wilt. Remove and set aside.

When the ragù is ready, discard the bay leaves and spoon some over the cooked pasta, enough to coat it well. Set aside to cool.

Preheat the oven to 180°C/160°C fan/350°F/gas mark 4.

When you're ready to construct the pie, dust a work surface with flour and roll out the pastry to 3mm (⅛in) thick and large enough to line and cover a cast-iron pan; ours is 25cm (10in) in diameter. Place a circle of greaseproof paper in the bottom of the pan and grease the sides with olive oil. Carefully line the pan with the pastry. Leave it draping over the edges of the pan so you can fold it over the top once filled.

Spoon in the pasta and spread out evenly, then carefully cover with the béchamel sauce and the grated cheese. Scatter over the chard and the butternut squash, then the sausage pieces. Top with the remaining ragù. Fold the edges of the pastry over the top of the pie, using offcuts to cover any gaps. Put the lid on the pan and cook for 1 hour, then remove the lid and cook for a further 20 minutes until the top is golden.

Allow the pie to cool in the pan for 20 minutes. Use a palette knife to loosen the sides of the pie before carefully inverting it on to a serving plate or board. Leave to cool for another 10 minutes before cutting. Serve with a big green salad and a large glass of red.

MUSHROOM & STOUT STEAMED PUD

Move aside nut roast, this is your new go-to for long Sunday lunches! A plant-based version of a traditional steak and kidney pudding, the stout and chocolate envelop the mushrooms in a decadently dark gravy packed with umami flavours.

1 quantity of vegan suet pastry (page 28), made with the addition of ¾ teaspoon bicarbonate of soda

plain flour, for dusting

FOR THE FILLING

12 shallots, halved

5 tablespoons olive oil, plus extra for greasing

900g (2lb) mixed mushrooms (we used oyster, baby king oyster and shiitake), chopped into large chunks

4 large sprigs of thyme, leaves picked

250–350ml (9–12fl oz) stout

2 garlic cloves, finely chopped

1 sprig of rosemary

2 bay leaves

½ teaspoon nutritional yeast flakes

1 teaspoon Dijon mustard

1 square of dairy-free dark chocolate (85% cocoa solids)

1 tablespoon coconut aminos

a pinch of demerara sugar (to taste)

1 tablespoon cornflour

salt and freshly ground black pepper

Preheat the oven to 200°C/180°C fan/400°F/gas mark 6.

Put the halved shallots on a baking tray, drizzle with 1 tablespoon of the oil and season with salt and pepper. Roast the shallots for 10 minutes. Remove from the oven and add the mushrooms. Spread out the mushrooms on top of the semi-cooked shallots, season with salt and pepper, and drizzle with 3 tablespoons of the olive oil. Sprinkle over half of the thyme. Roast the mushrooms and shallots for 10 minutes, checking and turning halfway. Set aside to cool. It may be that some liquid leaks from the mushrooms – in this case, strain it off and place in a jug. Pour the stout into the jug to make up the total of volume of liquid to 350ml (12fl oz).

Heat the remaining tablespoon of oil in a pan, add the chopped garlic and cook for a few minutes until nicely aromatic, taking care not to allow it to brown. Add the rosemary, bay leaves and remaining thyme, along with the stout mixture, yeast flakes and Dijon mustard. Cook for 20 minutes or until the sauce has reduced by at least half. Strain the liquid to remove the herbs and return the sauce to the pan. Stir in the square of chocolate and the coconut aminos. Add demerara sugar, to taste, along with salt and pepper. Stir together the cornflour and a splash of the sauce in a bowl to make a smooth paste. Add this to the sauce and cook until nicely thickened. Remove the pan from the heat and add the cooled shallots and mushrooms to the sauce and mix together to coat all the vegetables.

Generously grease a 1.5-litre (2¾-pint) pudding basin with oil and cut a piece of greaseproof paper to fit the base. Oil this too. Lightly flour the work surface and set aside a ball of pastry to use for the lid. Roll out the remaining dough into a 3mm (⅛in) thick circle. To line the basin, fold the circle in half and then in half again before lifting it in with the pointed end of the pastry downwards. Unfold in the basin, moulding the dough to the basin, pressing down so the edges are all the same thickness and to patch up any breaks. Trim off any excess dough.

Tip the mushrooms and shallots into the pastry-lined basin. Roll out the pastry lid, moisten the edges with water, arrange over the basin and squeeze the lid and the edges together to seal. Cut a piece of greaseproof paper and foil to fit over the basin. Lay the foil on top of the paper and fold a pleat in the middle so there is space for the pudding to puff up a bit. Cover the basin with the paper and foil (paper side down). Secure with string under the rim. Cut off any excess greaseproof paper. Make a string handle to lift up the pudding.

Put the basin into a large saucepan and pour in water halfway up the sides. Cover the pan and simmer for 2 hours. Check the water from time to time to ensure it continues to be halfway up the sides – topping up occasionally. Carefully remove the pudding from the saucepan and turn it out on to a serving plate. Serve hot in slices.

MINTY LAMB PIE

A gnarly, no-nonsense version of the Pieminister original: slow-cooked lamb shank with redcurrant and mint sauce and lovely chunks of veg. Serve up with some minty mushy peas and boiled new potatoes.

½ **portion of suet pastry (page 28 or use shortcrust, page 27)**

1 **free-range egg, beaten**

plain flour, for dusting

FOR THE FILLING

4 tablespoons olive oil

4 lamb shanks

a knob of butter

1 onion, chopped

2 garlic cloves, chopped

2 tablespoons balsamic vinegar

200ml (7fl oz) red wine

250ml (9fl oz) beef stock

2 bay leaves

a few sprigs of thyme, leaves picked

1 carrot, washed and chopped

1 celery stick, chopped

300g (10½oz) swede, peeled and cut into cubes

100g (3½oz) frozen peas

1½ tablespoons redcurrant jelly

1 tablespoon mint sauce

1–2 teaspoons cornflour

a small handful of chopped mint

salt and freshly ground black pepper

Heat 3 tablespoons of the olive oil in a large pan, add the lamb shanks and season with salt and pepper. Brown the shanks on all sides, turning to ensure that they are evenly coloured. Remove from the pan.

Add the remaining tablespoon of oil and the knob of butter to the pan. Fry the onion over a low heat for 5–8 minutes until softened. Add the garlic and balsamic vinegar and cook for a few minutes, then return the lamb to the pan and pour in the red wine and stock. Tuck the bay leaves in and sprinkle in the thyme leaves. Bring to a low simmer, cover with the lid and cook for about 2½ hours, or until the shank meat is beautifully tender and offers little resistance when poked with a knife. Turn the shanks over from time to time while cooking.

Add the carrot, celery and swede to the pan and cook for a further 20 minutes. Remove the shanks from the pan and set aside. Add the frozen peas to the pan along with the redcurrant jelly and mint sauce. Cook for a few minutes and then strain about 150ml (5fl oz) of the liquid into a measuring jug to set aside for making gravy. You may need to strain a bit more off, depending on how much the sauce has thickened after the long cook.

Mix 1 teaspoon of the cornflour with a little of the cooking liquid in a small bowl and then stir this into the pan and cook until nicely thickened. You may need to stir in another teaspoon of the cornflour if the sauce hasn't thickened enough. Remove from the heat, stir in the chopped mint and leave the sauce to cool.

Spoon the lamb and veg into a large pie dish (we used a 22cm/8½in one), flaking a little of the meat into the veg and allowing the bones to stick up.

Dust a work surface with flour and roll out the suet pastry to fit the dish. Carefully top the pie with it, pushing down on to the bones so that they poke through the lid. Place in the fridge for 20 minutes.

Preheat the oven to 200°C/180°C fan/400°F/gas mark 6. Brush the pies with beaten egg and then bake in the oven for about 30 minutes, or until browned and cooked through.

SAVE THIS RECIPE FOR A TIME WHEN YOU CAN GET GOOD, LOCAL LAMB (HOGGET OR MUTTON SHANKS WOULD WORK WELL TOO). A REGENERATIVE FARM WILL OFTEN PRODUCE BOTH BEEF AND LAMB BECAUSE CATTLE RIP UP LARGE CLUMPS OF VEGETATION WHILE SHEEP NIBBLE THE PASTURE SHORT. THIS COMBO MAKES FOR SUPER-HEALTHY SOIL AND A RICH BIODIVERSITY.

IT'S ALL DOWN TO THE EARTH

FARMING ON THE WILD SIDE

We hear a lot about what we need to do less of to release fewer greenhouse gases into the atmosphere. But what can we do more of, to draw those gases back down from the atmosphere? Sustainable farming is one of the most impactful ways to do this.

This is because healthy soil is amazing, storing masses of carbon in its broken down plant matter. In fact, soil stores more carbon than all the plants and trees in the world combined. In the UK, 70% of the land is farmed, most of which is by modern industrial farming methods that doesn't treat soil well. By making the process regenerative, the potential to improve soil health, sequester more carbon and improve the surrounding wildlife is enormous.

Farm Wilder works with a group of farms doing just this; working with the land and wildlife, not against it. We joined founders Tim Martin and Luke Dale-Harris at Great Hound Tor in Devon where Cat Frampton farms cattle and sheep on East Dartmoor.

We were struck by the diverse beauty of Cat's land as we set out to meet her cows — these were not fields as such, more a mix of woodland, marshland and moorland. The gateways between the thick hedgerows are too narrow for modern tractors, which isn't a problem for Cat. Disturbing the land with machinery is a no-no on a regenerative farm such as Great Hound Tor anyway.

Every 2–3 days, Cat moves the cows to graze on fresh new pasture, while the just-grazed area is left for weeks to regenerate. The cows enjoy an abundant variety of plants to graze on, full of nutrients grown without the need for fertilizer. And because the pastures are never grazed long enough to be 'stripped bare' (far from it), the wild plants, birds and insects thrive too.

And this isn't just brilliant for biodiversity, there's another bonus to all of this — it's healthier too! Regenerative farmers graze pastures with a far wider range of herbs, legumes and grasses that don't need chemical fertilizers — and this greater variety of plants leads to meat with higher levels of minerals and vitamins, with less saturated fat and with more beneficial fatty acids.

Our governments know they need to make radical changes to save our soil and have the massive task of turning the mighty agricultural ship around.

But we can all help speed up change through our consumer choices and by spreading the word. Buy from regenerative farms — or look for assurance that your meat and dairy produce is 100% pasture- or grass-fed and/or organic (which includes many of the same sustainable practices).

Meeting Tim and Luke from Farm Wilder and Cat from Great Hound Tor inspired the Wild Farm Pudding overleaf. One of a small number of beef recipes in this book, it's a feast day recipe for a special occasion. One to splash out on high-welfare, regeneratively farmed beef for.

After all, if we want farmers to transition to a more sustainable way of farming, we need to support them. Properly indulgent, this pudding pie also contains local oysters. There aren't many fish species that can be considered truly sustainable these days, but oysters, mussels and other bivalve shellfish are the regeneratively farmed foods of the sea!

WILD FARM PUDDING

Farm Wilder suggested we create a pie based on this classic Victorian recipe. Properly indulgent, it uses oysters to bulk out the beef. They're a great addition because they mean we can use less beef but they're also the regeneratively farmed food of the sea, cleaning the water and even sequestering carbon!

½ **portion of suet pastry (page 28), made with the addition of ½ teaspoon of bicarbonate of soda**

plain flour, for dusting

2 tablsepoons grated horseradish (optional)

butter, for greasing

FOR THE FILLING

3 tablespoons olive oil

3 shallots, cut into thin rings

2 garlic cloves, sliced

2 carrots, washed, trimmed and diced

800g (1lb 12oz) beef cheek, sinew and fat trimmed, cut into 2–3cm (¾–1¼in) cubes

1 tablespoon tomato purée

4 tablespoons sherry vinegar

200ml (7fl oz) red wine

300ml (10fl oz) beef stock

1 tablespoon Worcestershire sauce

1 bouquet garni

½ small celeriac, peeled and cut into 1.5cm (5/8in) cubes

10 fresh oysters, shucked and juices reserved

salt and freshly ground black pepper

Heat 1 tablespoon of the oil in a large pan over a medium heat. Add the shallots and cook until slightly softened. Add the garlic and carrots and cook for 5 minutes until softened. Remove from the pan and set aside.

Heat 2 tablespoons of oil in the pan. Add the beef cheek and cook for about 20 minutes, turning so it browns all over. Add the tomato purée and cook for a minute, then add the sherry vinegar. When the liquid has evaporated, pour in the red wine and reduce the liquid by half. Add the beef stock, Worcestershire sauce, bouquet garni and cooked vegetables to the pan. Season with salt and pepper.

Reduce the heat to low, cover with a lid and cook for 4½ hours, stirring occasionally. The beef should be very tender. Add the celeriac 30 minutes before the end of the cooking time, along with a splash of water if the sauce has depleted too much. Once cooked, most of the sauce should have been absorbed into the meat and celeriac. Leave to cool.

Butter a 1-litre (1¾-pint) pudding basin, cut a piece of greaseproof paper to fit the base and butter that too. Flour a work surface and press the grated horseradish into the pastry as you roll it, to evenly distribute it – it will make the pastry a bit moister but just sprinkle over a little flour as you go. Set aside a ball of pastry to use for the lid. Roll the rest of the dough into a 2mm (1/16in) thick circle. To line the basin, fold the pastry circle in half and then in half again before lifting it in with the pointed end of the pastry downwards. Unfold in the basin, moulding the dough to the basin, pressing down so the edges are all the same thickness and to patch up any breaks. Trim off any excess dough.

Gently stir the oysters and their juices into the cooled meat mixture, ensuring that they are evenly distributed. Fill the pastry-lined basin with the cooled filling, then roll out the lid and arrange it over the rim of the basin. Moisten the edges of the pastry with water and seal the dough together.

Cut a piece of greaseproof paper and foil to fit over the basin. Lay the foil on top of the paper and fold a pleat in the middle so that there is space for the pudding to puff up a bit. Cover the basin with the paper and foil, paper-side down. Secure with string under the rim. Cut off any excess paper. Make a string handle to lift the pudding.

Put the basin into a large saucepan and pour in water halfway up the sides. Cover the pan and simmer for 1 hour. Check the water level in the pan from time to time to ensure it continues to be halfway up the sides – topping up occasionally.

Using the string handle, carefully remove the pudding from the saucepan and turn it out on to a serving plate. Serve hot in slices.

SHALLOTA ROOTS

A rootin' tootin' roast veg pie, the red onions, butternut squash, celery and garlic are all melded together along with a handful of barley in an umami-bomb gravy. The sort of thing to serve up as the autumn evenings draw in.

½ **portion of vegan suet pastry (page 28)**

plain flour, for dusting

FOR THE FILLING

6 small red onions, halved and then sliced into wedges

½ butternut squash (about 300g/10½oz), peeled and cut into chunks

4 celery sticks, cut into chunks

2 tablespoons apple cider vinegar

1 tablespoon maple syrup

3 tablespoons olive oil, plus extra for greasing

1 garlic bulb, broken into cloves still in skins)

1 leek, sliced

½ portion of vegan gravy (page 180)

5cm (2in) piece of fresh ginger, sliced

1½ teaspoons barley miso paste

40g (1½oz) pearl barley, rinsed

salt and freshly ground black pepper

Preheat the oven to 200°C/180°C fan/400°F/gas mark 6.

Put the onions, butternut squash and celery in a single layer in two ovenproof dishes. Combine the cider vinegar, maple syrup and 2 tablespoons of the olive oil in a small bowl and mix together. Pour the mixture over the vegetables and roast for 30 minutes, then add the whole garlic cloves to the dish and cook for a further 15 minutes.

Heat the remaining tablespoon of olive oil in a large pan and fry the leek until softened, but not browned. Add the gravy to the pan with the ginger slices, miso and pearl barley. Stir to combine. Simmer for 15 minutes until nicely thickened, stirring from time to time.

Once the garlic has cooled, slip the roasted garlic out of the peel. Tip all the vegetables into the pan, including the garlic, and simmer for a further 5 minutes. Remove from the heat and discard the pieces of ginger. Leave the filling to cool.

Brush a pie dish (we used a 22cm/8½in round pie tin) with oil. Lightly flour a clean work surface and set aside a small ball of the pastry for a lid. Roll out the pastry to 3mm (⅛in) thick and line the pie dish with the pastry, trimming off any excess. Fill the pie case with the filling. Roll out a lid for the pie, put a little water around the pastry rim and then cover the filling with the lid and press the edges together to crimp. Place the pie in the fridge for at least 30 minutes, or until you are ready to cook it.

Preheat the oven to 200°C/180°C fan/400°F/gas mark 6 while the pie is chilling.

Brush the top of the pie with a little oil and bake for 30–35 minutes or until browned and cooked through. Serve in slices.

RESERVE THE SEEDS FROM YOUR BUTTERNUT SQUASH TO MAKE A DELICIOUS SNACK. SIMPLY DRIZZLE WITH OLIVE OIL IN A SMALL OVEN TRAY AND ROAST IN AN OVEN PREHEATED TO 180°C/160°C FAN/350°F/GAS MARK 4 FOR 15 MINUTES UNTIL CRUNCHY, BUT NOT TOO BROWNED.

MOOLESS & BLUELESS

The vegan version of our steak and Stilton pie, this dish has the power to persuade the most carnivorous of beef eaters that plant-based eating is for them!

½ **portion of vegan shortcrust pastry (page 27)**

½ **portion of vegan suet pastry (page 28)**

a little oat milk

FOR THE FILLING

25g (1oz) dried porcini mushrooms

1 tablespoon organic rapeseed oil

1 onion, finely diced

3 carrots, washed and diced

2 celery sticks, diced

3 garlic cloves, crushed

150g (5½oz) oyster mushrooms, chopped

800g (1lb 12oz) jackfruit, drained

1 tablespoon plain flour, plus extra for dusting

1 tablespoon tomato purée

1 tablespoon vegan Worcestershire sauce

2 teaspoons brown sugar

330ml (11fl oz) porter-style beer

1 sprig of rosemary

1 sprig of thyme

1 bay leaf

200g (7oz) plant-based blue cheese, chopped

salt and freshly ground black pepper

chopped parsley, to serve

Put the porcini mushrooms into a bowl and cover with boiling water. Set aside to steep.

Heat the oil in a large heavy-based saucepan and gently cook the onion, carrots and celery for 8–10 minutes until softened. Increase the heat to medium and add the garlic and oyster mushrooms and, when they start to colour, stir in the jackfruit.

Drain the porcini mushrooms, reserving the liquor, chop and add to the pan. Sprinkle over the flour and cook, stirring for 1 minute then stir in the tomato purée, Worcestershire sauce and brown sugar. Slowly add the mushroom liquor, stirring all the time, then add the porter. Throw in the herbs, season well and bring to a simmer. Cook for 40 minutes until the sauce has thickened and the vegetables are all soft. Set aside to cool.

Dust a work surface with flour and roll out the shortcrust pastry to 3mm (⅛in) thick and large enough to fit a large pie dish; ours is 23cm (9in). Drape the pastry into the dish, gently shaping into the corners and trim off the excess.

Stir the chunks of cheese into the jackfruit mixture, then spoon into the pastry case and level. Roll out the suet pastry to 3mm (⅛in) thick, to fit the top of the pie dish. Brush the edges of the shortcrust with a little oat milk, then lay the suet crust over the top. Trim the excess, then crimp the edges together to seal. Brush the top of the pie with oat milk and use any pastry offcuts to decorate the top, then cut a small steam hole in the top.

Preheat the oven to 200°C/180°C fan/400°F/gas mark 6 while you refrigerate the pie. Bake for 40 minutes until the top is browned. Leave to stand for 10 minutes and serve with a sprinkling of parsley.

VEGAN CHEESE HAS COME A LONG WAY IN RECENT YEARS, WITH ARTISANAL PRODUCERS POPPING UP EVERYWHERE. TRY AS MANY AS YOU CAN UNTIL YOU FIND ONE THAT HITS THE SPOT!

FRANK'S BIRIYANI

Our friends at Frank Water provide safe, sustainable solutions to combat water scarcity in some of the world's poorest communities, taking simple steps to ensure that precious groundwater stores are replenished. From planting trees to digging lakes, they're helping create water-secure futures for thousands of people across Nepal and Northern India – the birthplace of the biryani – so we dedicate this pie to them and the great work they do.

1 portion of vegan mighty white pastry (page 24)

plain flour, for dusting

plant-based milk, for brushing

FOR THE FILLING

2 tablespoons vegetable oil, plus extra for greasing

1 onion, sliced

½ teaspoon fennel seeds

½ teaspoon nigella seeds

½ teaspoon cumin seeds

1–2 red chillies, deseeded and finely chopped (to taste)

150g (5½oz) peeled celeriac, cut into 1.5cm (5/8in) cubes

2 small baby aubergines, sliced

150g (5½oz) cauliflower, cut into florets

1 medium tomato, chopped

40g (1½oz) dried fruit, such as sultanas and raisins

a small handful of coriander, chopped

a small handful of mint, chopped

30g (1oz) cashews, toasted

salt

FOR THE RICE

150g (5½oz) basmati rice

3 cloves

1 bay leaf

3 cardamom pods, crushed

1 small cinnamon stick

¼ teaspoon ground turmeric

a generous pinch of salt

2 tablespoons rosewater

Heat 1 tablespoon of the oil in a pan and fry the onion for 5–8 minutes until it becomes translucent. Add the fennel, nigella and cumin seeds and the chillies and fry for a couple of minutes. Add the remaining tablespoon of oil, the celeriac, aubergine and a pinch of salt. Cover and cook over a low heat (do not add any water) for 5 minutes or so, then add the cauliflower. After it's nicely coated in everything and softened, add the tomato. Stir in the dried fruit and set aside to cool.

To make the rice, put the rice, cloves, bay leaf, crushed cardamom pods, cinnamon stick, turmeric and salt in a saucepan with 375ml (13fl oz) water. Bring to the boil, then cover with a lid carefully wrapped in a tea towel (this will absorb extra liquid), reduce the heat and simmer for about 10 minutes until the liquid has all absorbed. The rice can still have a little bite. Remove the bay leaf and spices and set the rice aside to cool. Once cool, stir in the rosewater.

Grease a pie dish with a little oil. Dust a work surface with flour and set aside a third of the pastry for the lid. Roll out the remaining pastry to 3mm (⅛in) thick and use it to line a deep 22cm (8½in) pie dish, trimming the excess. Spoon in one third of the rice, cover with half of the vegetables and sprinkle with half of the fresh coriander and mint. Repeat these layers again and sprinkle over the toasted cashews. Finally, top with the remaining rice. Brush the edges of the pastry base with a little plant-based milk. Roll out the remaining pastry to form a lid. Brush the edges of the pie with a little water, then drape the lid over the top. Crimp the edges to seal and trim away any excess. Make a hole in the top. Place in the fridge for at least 1 hour until you are ready to cook.

Preheat the oven to 200°C/180°C fan/400°F/gas mark 6. Brush the pastry with oil and bake for 40 minutes until golden brown and cooked through. Cover with a sheet of foil if the pie is starting to look too brown before the cooking time is up. Great served with lime pickle, mango chutney, raita and a green salad.

PEAS & LOVE

USE WHATEVER VEGETABLES NEED EATING. TRY COURGETTES, PEAS, GREEN BEANS – WHATEVER'S IN SEASON AND/OR IN YOUR FREEZER. AND IF YOU DON'T HAVE ALL THE SPICES MENTIONED EITHER, FEEL FREE TO IMPROVISE!

#

FKA Moo Dog, when we used to make it with a 'punky' ale from a small Scottish craft brewer...! Nowadays there are so many amazing independent breweries about, choose one you want to support when you make this pie. Full-bodied and flavoursome, this pie's a great entertainer, perfect for dinner parties or an alternative to a Sunday roast. A pie of this size means there's a big blank canvas of a lid for your pastry art, so leave time to get creative before you pop the whole thing in the oven.

½ **portion of shortcrust pastry (page 27)**

½ **portion of suet pastry (page 28)**

1 free-range egg, beaten

plain flour, for dusting

FOR THE FILLING

1 tablespoon organic rapeseed oil

600g (1lb 5oz) beef pieces, such as chuck or braising steak

300g (10½oz) smoked lardons

1 onion, finely diced

3 carrots, washed and diced

2 celery sticks, diced

3 garlic cloves, crushed

1 tablespoon plain flour

1 tablespoon tomato purée

1 tablespoon Worcestershire sauce

2 teaspoons English mustard powder

1 tablespoon black treacle

500ml (18fl oz) good-quality beef stock

250ml (9fl oz) hoppy ale

1 tablespoon green peppercorns, crushed

1 tablespoon rosemary leaves, chopped

2 bay leaves

salt and freshly ground black pepper

Heat the oil in a large, heavy-based ovenproof pan with a lid and brown the beef on all sides. Remove from the pan with a slotted spoon and set aside. Cook the lardons in the same pan until they're brown too. Take them out of the pan and set aside with the beef. Reduce the heat to medium–low and gently cook the onion, carrots, celery and garlic for 8–10 minutes with the lid on.

Sprinkle over the flour and cook, stirring for 1 minute, then stir in the tomato purée, Worcestershire sauce, mustard powder and treacle. Slowly add the stock and ale, stirring all the time. Add the peppercorns and herbs, season well and bring to a simmer.

Preheat the oven to 160°C/140°C fan/325°F/gas mark 3.

Return the beef and lardons to the pan and cook in the oven, with the lid on, for 2–3 hours until the meat is very tender. Once cooked, set aside to cool.

Dust a work surface with flour and roll out the shortcrust pastry to 3mm (⅛in) thick and large enough to fit a large pie dish; ours is 23cm (9in). Drape it into the dish, gently shaping into the corners and trim off the excess. Spoon the beef filling into the pastry case and level.

Roll out the suet pastry to 3mm (⅛in) thick, to fit the top of the pie dish. Brush the edges of the shortcrust with a little beaten egg, then lay the suet pastry over the top. Trim the excess, then crimp the edges together to seal. Brush the top of the pie with beaten egg, use any offcuts to decorate, and cut a small steam hole in the top. Transfer to the fridge to rest.

Preheat the oven to 200°C/180°C fan/400°F/gas mark 6 while you refrigerate the pie.

Bake the pie for 40 minutes until the top is browned. Leave to stand for 10 minutes before serving.

TOP TIP!

WHEN TRYING TO REDUCE THE AMOUNT OF BEEF YOU EAT, IT'S WORTH SAVING UP FOR THE BEST MEAT YOU CAN AFFORD AND CELEBRATING IT WITH AN EVENT PIE LIKE THIS BEAUTY.

THE MEANING OF GLEANING

TAKING ACTION TO STOP THE ROT

Gleaning, the gathering of residual crops left after a harvest, goes back centuries. But at a time when one third of all food grown globally is wasted, has this ancient practice ever been as pertinent as it is today?

A (literally) grassroots way to fight food waste and hunger on a local scale, the good news is that a volunteer-led gleaning movement is picking up pace.

Working with both farmers and food banks, it's a win-win for everyone, ensuring perfectly good food that was destined to rot gets to those that need it the most.

Whether it's deemed not up to supermarket standards or simply left in fields due to labour shortages, gleaners are the heroes who swoop in and harvest food before it's too late.

One such hero is Nick Haigh, who's been running the Avon Gleaning Network since 2020. When news of surplus salad and veg reached us via the gleaning grapevine, we went along to a farm in Somerset and got digging and snipping. In just a couple of hours we'd swept through the fields, filling boxes with Kohlrabi, spinach, lettuce, chard and beetroot. Once we'd packed and portioned it all, it was ready to be distributed to vulnerable people through food banks and community projects in the nearby city of Bath.

To see the boxes fill up fast with fresh and nutritious produce destined for the most deserving of causes felt good.

Millions of tonnes of food is wasted on farms every year, but if the new gleaning revolution keeps growing, it will go some way to ensure that the stuff that we grow ends up where it belongs, on someone's dinner plate.

AUBERGINE PARMESAN PIE

We've taken a classic Italian melanzane alla parmigiana recipe and dropped it into a crisp pastry. One bite and you'll be transported to Southern Italy (not literally, unfortunately. Sorry).

1 portion of olive oil pastry (page 25)

1 free-range egg, beaten

plain flour, for dusting

olive oil, for drizzling, greasing and cooking

FOR THE FILLING

750g (1lb 10oz) tomatoes, halved

a pinch of sugar

1 small onion, finely chopped

2 garlic cloves, finely chopped

1 chipotle chilli, soaked in warm water for 20 minutes

3 aubergines, cut into 5mm (¼in) circles

a knob of butter

125g (4½oz) mozzarella, sliced

150g (5½oz) Parmesan, grated (or vegetarian alternative)

a handful of basil leaves

salt and freshly ground black pepper

Preheat the oven to 200°C/180°C fan/400°F/gas mark 6 and lightly oil a roasting tin.

To make the filling, put the tomatoes, cut-side up, in the prepared tin, then sprinkle with salt, pepper and sugar. Drizzle over more olive oil and roast for 20 minutes.

Add the chopped onion and garlic to the tomatoes and roast for another 20 minutes or so. Keep checking to be sure that nothing is burning.

Remove from the oven, cool until easy to handle, and then tip into a food processor or blender. Drain and chop the soaked chilli and then add to the tomatoes. Add a little water if it is looking too thick. Leave to cool.

Spread out the aubergine circles in a greased roasting tin or baking tray (you may need to use two trays) and drizzle with oil. Roast for 20 minutes, turning the slices halfway through cooking. Hopefully you can do this while the tomatoes are in the oven, but if you don't have enough shelves in your oven to do this, you may need to cook the veg in batches (another option is to grill or griddle the aubergine). Remove and leave the aubergine to cool.

If you have turned the oven off, make sure it is preheated to 200°C/180°C fan/400°F/gas mark 6.

Dust a work surface with flour and flatten the dough on the floured surface. Dust the top with flour and then roll it out, dusting with more flour and flipping the dough over from time to time until it is about 3mm (⅛in) thick.

Grease a 30cm (12in) pie dish generously with both butter and olive oil. Lay the dough in the dish, draping any extra dough over the sides.

Put a layer of the tomato sauce over the dough, top with a layer of aubergine circles, dot over a third of the mozzarella, a layer of the sauce, a little Parmesan and a few torn basil leaves.

Repeat to use up all the ingredients, finishing with a layer of the tomato sauce topped with Parmesan and basil. With a sharp knife, slice off the edges of the pastry and then crimp the edges, taking real care to make sure that the edges are as thin as the base. Brush with the pastry edge with beaten egg. Bake for 40 minutes, or until cooked through and golden brown on top. Serve with more torn basil on top.

ANY DOUGH TRIMMINGS CAN BE MADE INTO RANDOM PASTA SHAPES AND COOKED IN A PAN OF BOILING, SALTED WATER ANOTHER DAY.

DOLPHIN NOSE

A dolphin friendly but NOT waistline friendly dish. We strongly advise you to only eat dauphinoise potato pie on a day when you've definitely done your 20,000 steps. Don't attempt to do your 20,000 steps straight after eating it – you'll need a lie-down first...

½ **portion of suet pastry (page 28)**

plain flour, for dusting

FOR THE FILLING

1 tablespoon organic rapeseed oil

1 large onion, thinly sliced

2 garlic cloves, sliced

200g (7oz) spring greens or cabbage, tough stems removed, and leaves shredded

300ml (10fl oz) double cream

100ml (3½fl oz) milk

¼ nutmeg, grated

3 sprigs of thyme

500g (1lb 2oz) waxy potatoes, thinly sliced

200g (7oz) Taleggio cheese, sliced

1 teaspoon Aleppo pepper

salt and freshly ground black pepper

Heat the oil in a heavy-based frying pan and gently cook the onion for 5–8 minutes until softened. Add the garlic and then the greens, season and stir to combine, coating everything in oil. Put the lid on the pan and gently steam for 3–5 minutes until the greens are wilted. Remove from the heat.

Put the cream and milk into a large pan with the grated nutmeg and thyme, season and gently heat, but do not boil. When the pan is steaming, add the potato slices and continue to warm until the potatoes start to soften. Carefully lift out the potatoes with a slotted spoon and set aside to cool.

Continue to warm the milk gently until it's reduced by half. Cover the surface with a pan lid or plate and set aside to cool.

When you are ready to assemble the pies, dust a work surface with flour and roll out the pastry to about 3mm (⅛in) thick. Grease two 225g (8oz) pie dishes and line each one with pastry, trimming off the excess. Put a layer of potato slices in the bottom of each pie, then a layer of greens and dot over the cheese. Spoon some of the reduced cream mixture over and repeat until both pies are full, finishing with a layer of potatoes. Place in the fridge for at least 20 minutes.

Preheat the oven to 200°C/180°C fan/400°F/gas mark 6.

Bake the pies in the oven for 35–40 minutes, or until golden-brown. Sprinkle with a little Aleppo pepper to serve.

DUTCH COURAGE APPLE PIE

This pie pays homage to our Dutch friend, Robert, who's been a huge source of advice and encouragement to us both over the last 10 years. Not only has he helped whip a couple of feckless punks into shape, but he's also given us a great excuse to visit Amsterdam, where we've munched on many a Bitterballen (Dutch meatball) followed by the odd Dutch apple pie. We've celebrated our Anglo–Dutch friendship by adding a dash of Somerset brandy.

1/3 portion of brown butter pastry (page 19)

FOR THE CRUMBLE TOPPING

85g (3oz) unsalted butter, plus extra for greasing

1 teaspoon lemon juice

100g (3½oz) soft light brown sugar

100g (3½oz) plain flour, plus extra for dusting

¼ teaspoon freshly ground nutmeg

a pinch of ground cloves

a pinch of salt

1½ tablespoons Somerset cider brandy

FOR THE FILLING

800g (1lb 12oz) apples, thinly sliced

2 tablespoons melted butter

70g (2½oz) granulated sugar

40g (1½oz) plain flour

2 tablespoons Somerset cider brandy

1½ teaspoons ground cinnamon

pinch of freshly grated nutmeg

To make the topping, first brown the butter. Put the butter in a small pan over a medium heat. Swirl the pan a little – the whey of the butter will drop to the bottom of the pan and, once the colour becomes golden toffee (not dark brown), quickly remove from the heat and add the lemon juice to fix the colour. Pour into a Pyrex bowl and add the sugar, flour, nutmeg, cloves and salt. Pour in the Somerset cider brandy and stir to combine. Transfer to the fridge until ready to assemble the pie.

Preheat the oven to 200°C/180°C fan/400°F/gas mark 6.

To make the filling, toss together all the filling ingredients in a bowl. Grease a medium (22cm/8½in) round pie dish with butter.

Dust a work surface with flour and roll out the pastry to 3mm (⅛in) thick. Line the pie dish with the pastry, trimming off any excess. Place the apples into the pie in flat layers.

Remove the topping from the fridge and break it into clumps. Sprinkle the topping evenly over the pie. Bake the pie in the oven for about 45 minutes, or until golden brown and cooked through. Serve in slices.

WASTE NOT WANT NOT!

THERE'S NO NEED TO PEEL THE APPLES FOR THIS RECIPE – THE UNPEELED APPLES ADD COLOUR AND TEXTURE, SAVE TIME AND PRODUCE LESS FOOD WASTE.

RICE PUDDING PIE

Rice pudding and pies: two of the most comforting comfort foods ever created. Here we've married them together to create a dreamy, creamy pillow of fragrant perfection encased in a crust of nuttiness.

¾ portion of vegan almond and olive oil pastry (page 18)
plain flour, for dusting

FOR THE FILLING

130g (4½oz) pudding rice
750ml (1⅓ pints) full-fat milk
300ml (10fl oz) double cream
40g (1½oz) granulated sugar
1 bay leaf
1 sprig of thyme
a grating of nutmeg
thyme honey (local is always best), to serve

Preheat the oven to 160°C/140°C fan/325°F/gas mark 3.

While the pastry is resting in the fridge, put the rice, milk, cream, sugar and herbs into an ovenproof dish and stir briefly. Bake in the middle of the oven for 1¼–1½ hours, stirring occasionally. The rice pudding should be a spoon-able consistency, if it's still looking a bit sloppy return to the oven and check every 5 minutes.

Meanwhile, dust a work surface with flour and roll out the pastry to 3mm (⅛in) thick, then line a 20cm (8in) pie dish with the pastry. Return to the fridge for 30 minutes, then line the pastry with greaseproof paper, fill with baking beans or rice and blind bake in the top of the oven for 20 minutes until the pastry has dried. Set aside until the rice has cooked.

Increase the oven temperature to 180°C/160°C fan/350°F/gas mark 4. Spoon the cooked rice into the pastry case, discarding the bay and thyme stalks and sprinkle the top with nutmeg. Return to the oven for 30–40 minutes until the top has browned and the pudding just has a slight wobble in the middle. Don't worry if it looks a bit jiggly still, it will continue to set as it cools.

Leave to stand for 10 minutes, then cut into slices and serve drizzled with thyme honey.

Just as delicious hot or cold.

FOR A DELICIOUS PLANT-BASED PUD, JUST USE DAIRY ALTERNATIVES FOR THE MILK AND CREAM AND SERVE WITH EITHER INFUSED AGAVE SYRUP OR GO RETRO WITH SOME DOLLOPS OF RUNNY JAM. YUM.

SUBS, SIDES & SAUCES

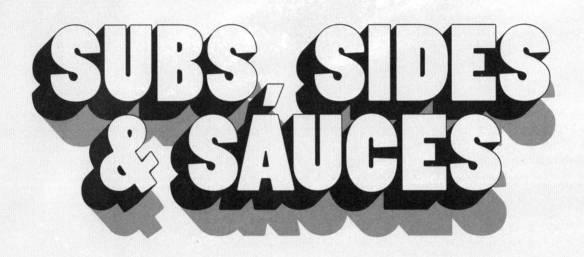

SOME OF OUR FAVOURITE
PLANT-BASED ALTERNATIVES
& SIGNATURE SAUCES

Spicy Tomato Ketchup

It's worth making a big batch of this sauce and filling up a bunch of sterilized bottles or jars, where it will keep, unopened, for months.

Makes approx. 2.5 litres (4½ pints)
Takes 1½ hours

30ml (1fl oz) vegetable oil
200g (7oz) onions, finely diced
4 teaspoons sea salt
30g (1oz) garlic, finely chopped
30g (1oz) fresh ginger, finely chopped
20g (¾oz) green chilli, deseeded and finely diced
20g (¾oz) red chilli, deseeded and finely diced
10g (¼oz) habanero chilli, deseeded and finely diced
1 teaspoon coarse black pepper
1 teaspoon ground cumin
1 teaspoon ground coriander
½ teaspoon red chilli flakes
a pinch of chipotle powder
3 teaspoons smoked paprika
400ml (14fl oz) cider vinegar
1 litre (1¾ pints) water
2 bay leaves
500ml (18fl oz) passata
200g (7oz) tomato purée
1 teaspoon caster sugar
50g (1¾oz) soft dark brown sugar
40g (1½oz) tamarind paste
2 teaspoons mustard seeds
2 teaspoons onion seeds
90g (3¼oz) cornflour

Heat the oil in a heavy-based pan with the onions and salt and cook over a gentle heat for about 10 minutes until the onions are soft and translucent. Add the garlic and ginger and continue to cook for 2 minutes. Add the chillies and the spices (except the onion and mustard seeds), then add the vinegar and water and simmer gently for 5 minutes before adding the bay leaves, passata, tomato purée and both sugars. Cover and cook slowly for about 1 hour.

Remove from the heat, then add the tamarind paste and whizz the sauce with a stick blender until smooth. Add the onion and mustard seeds.

In a jug or mug, combine the cornflour with a dash of water to make a thick paste, then add that to the sauce. Return the pan to the heat and stir for a few minutes while the sauce thickens, then remove from the heat.

Bottle the sauce, while hot, into sterilized bottles or jars (see page 181). Use a jam funnel to help fill the jars without spillage. It will keep for at least 6 months in a cool, dark place and, once opened, will last for up to 4 weeks in the fridge.

Fruity Brown Sauce

Like its spicy red friend, this will last for a few months in sterilized jars. So why not make a big batch and use as stocking fillers or last-minute 'thank you for looking after my cat' gifts?

Makes approx. 10 x 250ml (9fl oz) jars or bottles
Takes 1 hour

200g (7oz) onions, finely diced
400g (14oz) Bramley apples, peeled and diced
200g (7oz) dates, finely diced
4g (⅛oz) salt
½ teaspoon ground ginger
½ teaspoon ground cinnamon
a pinch of chipotle chilli powder
¼ teaspoon smoked paprika
¼ teaspoon cayenne pepper
230ml (8fl oz) malt vinegar
200g (7oz) demerara sugar
200g (7oz) soft dark brown sugar
80g (2¾oz) tomato purée
40g (1½oz) tamarind paste
400ml (14fl oz) cold water

In a large saucepan, gently cook the onions, apples, dates, salt and all the spices for 45 minutes, until the apples and onions are soft. Carefully blend the sauce with a stick blender, avoiding hot splashes, until completely smooth.

Add the vinegar and both sugars and cook for a further few minutes before adding the tomato purée, tamarind paste and cold water. Cook over a low heat for a further 30 minutes.

Bottle the sauce, while hot, into sterilized bottles or jars (see page 181). It will keep for at least 6 months in a cool, dark place and, once opened, will last for up to 4 weeks in the fridge.

PLANT-BASED GRAVY

This gravy is very rich and flavoursome. As well as a great gravy, it makes a good base for other sauces. You can try adding herbs, mustard, redcurrants, or even soya cream.

Serves 6–8
Takes 1 hour

1 tablespoon vegetable oil

200g (7oz) chestnut or field mushrooms, roughly chopped

½ carrot, washed and roughly chopped

1 large onion, roughly chopped

1 celery stick, roughly chopped

25g (1oz) plain flour

50ml (2fl oz) light soy sauce

1 teaspoon Worcestershire sauce

2 tablespoons balsamic vinegar

1.5 litres (2¾ pints) vegetable stock

1 garlic clove, whole

1 tablespoon redcurrant jelly

2 bay leaves

1 sprig of thyme

a pinch of black pepper

Heat the oil in a medium heavy-based pan. Add the mushrooms and brown them before adding the carrot, onion and celery. Keep the pan over a high heat so the vegetables colour and caramelize. Add the flour and stir continuously for just one minute, keeping a very close eye that it doesn't burn. Add the soy sauce, Worcestershire sauce and balsamic vinegar to the pan and stir with a wooden spatula to scrape all of the browned bits from the bottom of the pan. Continue to stir as you add the vegetable stock, then drop in the garlic clove, redcurrant jelly, bay leaves and thyme and simmer over a low heat for 30 minutes.

Mash up the veg a little with a potato masher. Taste and adjust the seasoning, then strain through a sieve into a clean pan and reduce by one third. Serve piping hot.

THIS GRAVY FREEZES WELL, SO SAVE ANY LEFTOVERS FOR A RAINY DAY. YOUR FUTURE SELF WILL THANK YOU!

PLANT-BASED BÉCHAMEL

Versatile and unbelievably good, this is the sort of recipe you'll return to again and again. It's perfect for all sorts of things, from lasagnes and moussakas to macaroni cheeses and mornays.

Makes enough to top a Moussaka for 6, such as our Mighty Aphrodite on page 99
Takes 5 minutes

300g (10½oz) silken tofu, well drained

30g (1oz) white miso paste

40g (1½oz) nutritional yeast

2 tablespoons olive oil

2 teaspoons onion granules

2 teaspoons garlic granules

¼ nutmeg, finely grated

salt and freshly ground black pepper

Put all the ingredients in a blender, season with salt and pepper and blend until smooth.

ROASTED JACKFRUIT

This is our chosen way to replace dark meat in a pie.

Makes enough for 2–4 pies, depending on the recipe
Takes 30 minutes

400g (14oz) can or packet of jackfruit

1 teaspoon nutritional yeast flakes

1 tablespoon miso paste (ideally brown rice miso, but red or white miso are good as well)

1 teaspoon polenta

Drain and dry the jackfruit with kitchen paper, place it in a bowl and tumble it with the remaining ingredients. Marinate in the fridge for 30 minutes.

Preheat the oven to 200°C/180°C fan/400°F/ gas mark 6.

Line a baking tray with greaseproof paper and spread the mix evenly over a baking tray. Cook for 20–25 minutes. It will dry out and roast up to intensify the flavours and create a good meaty texture.

PLANT-BASED CUSTARD

An all-purpose custard where a vanilla pod and seeds infuse flavour into oat milk the old-fashioned way. The smidge of turmeric gives this lovely creamy custard its bright colour.

Serves 4
Takes 20 minutes

250ml (9fl oz) unsweetened oat milk
⅓ vanilla pod
3 teaspoons cornflour
6 teaspoons golden caster sugar (or to taste)
a pinch of ground turmeric
150ml (5fl oz) oat cream

Put 225ml (8fl oz) of the oat milk in a saucepan. Scrape the vanilla pod to remove the seeds and place the pod and seeds in the pan with the milk. Bring to a simmer and then reduce the heat and leave the milk to infuse for 10 minutes.

Mix together the cornflour, the remaining 25ml (1fl oz) of oat milk, the sugar and turmeric in a small bowl. Don't overdo the turmeric – you want just enough to achieve the right colour.

Return the milk to the heat and whisk in the cornflour mixture while the milk is simmering. Once combined, whisk in the oat cream and allow to simmer until nicely thickened.

Remove the vanilla pod and serve.

This is best served right away, but any leftovers can be left in the fridge, covered with a piece of greaseproof paper to stop a film forming. It's pretty delicious cold, but if you want to reheat the custard, it may need a quick whisk to remove any lumps.

PLANT-BASED ICE CREAM

This sweet coconutty recipe doesn't need an ice-cream machine; you will, however, either need an electric whisk or very strong arms!

Serves 8
Takes 1 hour 10 minutes, plus 2–3 hours freezing

50g (1¾oz) coconut oil
200ml (7fl oz) coconut milk
150g (5½oz) caster sugar
½ vanilla pod
a pinch of sea salt
1 star anise
80ml (2½fl oz) aquafaba

Gently heat the coconut oil, coconut milk, caster sugar, vanilla, sea salt and star anise in a heavy-based pan and, once the sugar has dissolved, turn off the heat and let it steep for at least 1 hour before removing the star anise and the vanilla pod.

While you're waiting for the mix to cool, whisk up the aquafaba; this will take 7–8 minutes with an electric whisk – it will be ready when you can make soft peaks.

When the coconut mix has cooled, gently fold in the aquafaba and transfer to the freezer; stir the mix occasionally as it freezes. It will take a minimum of 2–3 hours in the freezer before it's firm enough to scoop.

To sterilize glass jars, simply wash with hot soapy water, then place on a baking tray in the oven at 140°C/120°C fan/275°F/gas mark 1 for about 15–20 minutes. You can use any glass jars or bottles with good-fitting lids. Make sure you fill and seal while the filling is hot.

JONNY Si's **CRYSTAL BALLS**

FOODIE FUTURES

HE SEES ALL!

LOVE FATE PASTRY!

SEE THE FUTURE

Hopefully this book's given you plenty of insight into sustainable eating – what to avoid and which foods and farming practices are better for the planet than others. With the Earth's population expected to reach 10 billion by 2050, we need to think about what we eat and how we produce it. What is exciting, is that there are people working away in sheds and laboratories across the world, to find sustainable ways to produce enough food for the future. Some of these are in action already, some are many years away from being fully operational.

HERE ARE A FEW THINGS WHICH ARE UNDER WAY AND A COUPLE OF OUR OWN PREDICTIONS FOR THE FUTURE OF FOOD.

HIGH-RISE URBAN FARMS

Urban farms have been around since the first cities emerged. However, as buildings have grown, and the focus has moved from farming to manufacturing, cities have relied on imports from further afield (literally). Times are changing, and Singapore, who import virtually all their food, is leading the way. With government support, farms are appearing on top of shopping malls, multi-story carparks, in schools, hotels and people's homes. In fact, almost anywhere that there is underutilized space. Whether it's hydroponically grown leafy greens, green-energy-driven rotating growing troughs in vertical greenhouses, or shipping containers in unused space growing mushrooms, they are all helping to deliver the city's 30/30 target (30% of the food consumed in the city to be grown in the city before 2030).

As we learned during our visit to LettUs Grow here in Bristol, crops grown in this way, without soil or pesticides, mean no nasty run-off polluting streams or upsetting biodiversity. Although these methods can be more labour- and energy-intensive, they can be far better controlled, meaning supply and demand can be carefully managed and aren't subject to weather conditions, improving the harvest, reducing

waste, and guaranteeing a far more stable supply chain. They can utilize green energy and reduce the carbon that's produced by traditional distribution methods.

São Paulo, Seoul and Tokyo all have their own urban farming initiatives and hopefully more will follow. So watch this space, or rather, watch those spaces in your local town or city!

Bug Pie Anyone?

Back in 2015 we launched a pie made with crickets called the Hopper. Partly to get some publicity, partly out of curiosity as to how realistic it would be to use bugs in making pies, and of course, to see how people would react to the idea. Well, we got in the paper, the pie tasted great, the customers, however, were a little harder to convince – perhaps we were before our time, in the UK anyway.

INSECTS HAVE BEEN EATEN FOR THOUSANDS OF YEARS BY HUMANS AND OVER 16,000 TYPES OF INSECT ARE STILL CONSUMED BY OVER 2 BILLION PEOPLE ACROSS 130 COUNTRIES TODAY.

So, you may ask, what's new? In western society the consumption of bugs is far from mainstream. Today the production of insects for human consumption is currently a $1 billion industry. And predicted to grow to $8 billion by 2030. Impressive growth, but a drop in the ocean compared to the $330 billion beef industry.

So why should we care and why should we take bugs seriously?

Firstly, they taste pretty good and have double the protein and produce 50% less carbon than chicken per 100g. Bugs are far more efficient at turning feed into protein than traditional livestock. As a result, they use six times less water and are faster to grow. They also don't need to be fed on mass produced monocrops which result in fertilizer run-off into our oceans, creating dead zones when no fish, coral or seaweed can survive, just algae.

Insect production also takes up far less land. Aspire, a firm in Canada who started large-scale cricket production in 2022, covers 12 acres of land. When in full-scale production, it will house 2.7 billion crickets at any one time and produce 12,000 tonnes of food a year packed full of nutrients and protein. The same land would house approximately 6 cows and produce only 72 tonnes of beef per year.

Along with vertical inner-city farming, production of bugs is easy to control and can be highly automated using artificial intelligence to ensure high yield production, meaning that they can be produced anywhere in the world and help feed people in countries with less access to water and animal feed.

So, what about perception in western society? Don't expect to be served a bowl of bugs in your local restaurant anytime soon. However, you could very likely see powders included in shakes or smoothies, or insect-protein-packed pasta or bread, delivering all-important nutrients into diets across the world.

THEIR TREATMENT SYSTEM IS SAID TO SAVE UP TO 98% OF THE WATER USED, WHILE USING AUTOMATED LIGHTING AND NUTRIENT DOSING SPECIFIC TO EACH PLANT SPECIES CURRENTLY IN PRODUCTION.

Sounds good doesn't it? And all the time these clever pods, which can work independently or linked together, will teach themselves how to save energy and predict yields while automating their crop selection and scheduling. Interstellar Labs aim to supply their pods for the sustainable lunar base and to future Mars exploration missions. A small step for man, but a huge step for machine kind!

GROUND CONTROL TO MAJOR TOMATO

In the International Space Station there is a vegetable production system called Veggie. So far in Veggie the crew members have grown lettuce, mustard, kale and cabbage and zinnia flowers.

Veggie is one of a few systems designed to help NASA better understand what's required to grow crops in space. This technology will ultimately supply astronauts with the essential vitamins and fresh produce to cope with deep space exploration.

While NASA's Veggie has been proving the viability of growing veg in space, back on Earth a company called Interstellar Labs has been busy creating AI-controlled bio-pods that can unlock the ability of doing this on a much larger scale.

Interstellar Labs' Luna pods are easy to assemble and transport. When in place they can create precise atmospheric conditions regardless of any extreme external conditions that you might find on other planets. Like LettUs Grow on page 122, the system uses mist to create the perfect conditions; it can currently be programmed to grow over 300 plants that can be used for either food or medicine. Their pods, that have been designed for use on Earth, also combine carbon capture and water-generating technology.

1.

2.

5.

6.

7.

11.

A BAKER'S DOZEN

FRESH FROM OUR BRISTOL BAKERY

It's these pie mixers, makers, packers and checkers and their workmates who keep the Pieminister pie wheels turning.

1. Sebastian, 2. Petruta 3. Jess
4. Thomas 5. Ebenezer 6. Mamadou
7. Gosia 8. Resham 9. Colin 10. Pawel
11. Casimiro 12. Beatriz 13. José

INDEX

ACKNOWLEDGEMENTS

Pieminister would like to thank Romany Simon, Jeni Hunsley, Ryan Thomas, Matt Sparkes, Rob Wicks, Alison Clarkson, Maria Perez, Ramona Andrews, Elayna Rudolphy, Sam Docker, Vicky Orchard, Joanna Copestick, Isabel Jessop, Yasia Williams and all those at Kyle Books.

Special thanks also go to Benedict Meade from Tempeh Meades, Eliza Reid from Bristol Greens Basket Scheme, Jack, Oscar and the rest of the team at LettUs Grow, Cat Frampton and family at Great Houndtor farm, Luke and Tim from Farm Wilder, Nick Haigh, Samantha Williamson, Skye Rose and the rest of the Avon Gleaning Network, Daisy Terry from Dusty Knuckle, all the recipe testers and tasters at Pieminister, Danny from Danny's Burgers, BoS Finesse, The Forge, Fierce and Noble, Eat Pictures Studio, Caroline Vail, Ginny Payne, Romy Viviani, Emily Feltham, Sophie Kirk, Jemillia Powell, Tess Rummer, Ned and Fina Simon, Lorna and Celeste Hogg, Judy Barrat, Frank Water, CALM and Forestry England.